Sang o the Nith

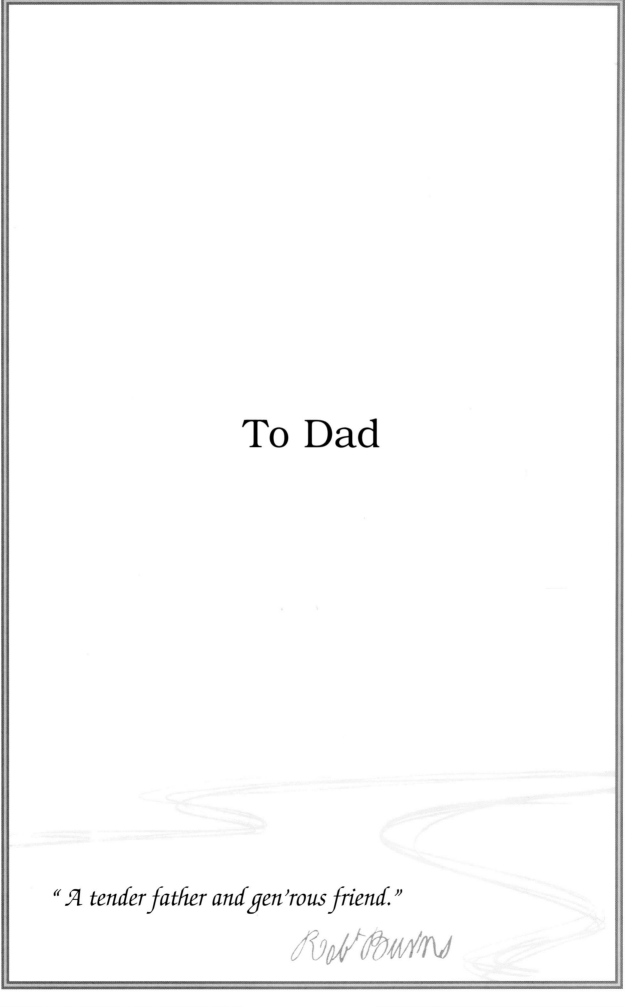

To Dad

" A tender father and gen'rous friend."

Robt Burns

Sang o the Nith

A poetic journey through
Dumfries and Galloway
to commemorate the bi-centenary
of the death of Robert Burns.

Compiled by

John Clark

Dumfries and Galloway
LIBRARIES
Information and Archives

First published in Dumfries, Scotland 1996
© Dumfries and Galloway Council
© Illustrations and text remain with their originators.

Watercolour and line illustration by
John Clark

Poetry by
The late John McDonald Clark
John Clark
Alan Clark BSc [Hons]

Introduction by Sandra M Wilson

Tribute by Sharon Clark

This book has been designed by Dumfries and Galloway Libraries, printed by Solway Offset Services, Dumfries and bound by Remploy Creative Products for

Dumfries and Galloway Libraries
Catherine Street, Dumfries DG1 1JB

ISBN 094628019-3

Dumfries and Galloway
LIBRARIES
Information and Archives

FOREWORD

In 1991 an exhibition of landscape painting, poetry and prints was held on the upper floor of James Thin's as part of the Dumfries Art Festival Fringe. A success in its own right the paintings and prints established John Clark as a successful artist whose paintings are much in demand. The success of the exhibition also inspired the artist to publish his father's poetry as a surprise anthology and the resultant book *Burns' Walk From The Memoried Past* was well received locally in Dumfries. Regretfully because of the surprise nature of the book some of the poetry was overlooked. The experience of putting together his father's work also inspired the artist to write poetry of his own, some of which was reworked into 'auld Scots' and Dumfries dialect by his father shortly before his death in August 1995. Along with the poems of Alan Clark, the result is for the most part a guided tour of the beautiful Dumfries and Galloway landscape where Robert Burns lived, worked and died. The area is seen through the eyes of three generations of local poets, not only as it is now but as it was seen through the eyes of the artist's father in the 1930's. Coupled with numerous illustrations, stories and snippets of local history, the book provides a unique opportunity to celebrate the bi-centenary of the death of Robert Burns by sharing the poetic interpretations, some serious, some humorous, written and compiled in his honour some two hundred years on by fellow Scots.

CONTENTS

INTRODUCTION

To set this book in context it is important to stress at the outset that this is not a book which deals exclusively with Robert Burns, although it appears in the bi-centennial year of his death. Rather this book is an eclectic mix of prose, poetry, painting and sketches, some of which relates directly to Burns and the area in which he lived, worked and died but also stems from a talented local family of the present day.

Throughout the book snippets of local history are included. These are intended to set the scene for the various poems and paintings. Locals and those from further afield alike may find this background useful.

The purpose of this introduction is to say a little about Robert Burns; a little about Dumfries and some of the places well known to Burns in his lifetime and a little about the Clark family whose work is showcased in this book.

Burns' Life before Dumfries

Robert Burns was born on the 25th of January in 1759. He was the eldest of seven children. His father, William Burness had come from Kincardineshire via Edinburgh to Ayrshire where he worked as a market gardener; his mother Agnes was an Ayrshire lass. During the first seven years of his life Burns lived in the cottage his father had built with his own hands in Alloway.

Although life was hard and money in short supply, Burns' father was dedicated to the principle of a sound education. As well as sending his son to school William Burness paid personal attention to some aspects of his son's education. Burns' mother introduced him to folk-song which undoubtedly influenced him greatly in later life.

In 1766 the family moved to Mount Oliphant Farm. This was not a success and they moved to another farm, Locklea near Tarbolton.

Gilbert Burns, the poet's youngest brother gives a moving account of life in the Burns' household around this period -

> *"To the buffetings of misfortune, we could only oppose hard labour and the most rigid economy. We lived very sparingly. For several years butchers' meat was a stranger in the house, while all members of the family exerted themselves to the utmost strength, and rather beyond it, in the labours of the farm. My brother at the age of thirteen assisted in threshing the crop of corn, and at fifteen was the principal labourer on the farm. For we had no hired servant male or female. The anguish of mind we felt at our tender years, under these straights and difficulties, was very great. To think of our father old (for he was now above fifty) broken down with long continued fatigues of his life, with a wife and five other children, and undeclining state of circumstances, these reflections produced in my brother's mind and mine sensations of the deepest distress."*

On his father's death, Burns and Gilbert took over the farm of Mossgiel. However success eluded the brothers and Burns began to despair of his having any future in farming, so much so that he made tentative plans to emigrate to Jamaica.

Ironically it was to raise funds for the voyage that Robert Burns decided to print his poems in Kilmarnock in 1786. This is the collection which became known as the *Kilmarnock Edition* and has been read throughout the world. Fortunately for Scotland Burns abandoned his plans to emigrate and, after the success of the first edition of his works, prepared to publish a second.

In 1788 Burns married Jean Armour and moved to Ellisland Farm near Dumfries. As well as farming he worked as an exciseman. However farming had long lost any real attraction for Burns and in 1791 he moved into Dumfries to take up full time employment in the excise. Dumfries and the surrounding countryside had now indeed become Burns' Country.

Burns and Dumfries

Robert Burns' first appearance in Dumfries had actually been in June 1787 shortly after the second edition of his poems was published. He came to be made an honorary burgess or freeman of the town. Dumfries had been quick off the mark in recognising the genius of the poet. Interestingly, in terms of this book, the Provost at the time was one William Clark.

The Burns family, Jean and Robert now with three children, took up residence in three small apartments on the second floor of a building

Burns' House

on the north side of Bank Street, known then as the Wee Vennel. After living there for about two years the family moved to a self- contained house in Mill Street. This is where Burns lived until his death. The street is now named after him - Burns' Street.

Dumfries seems to have been acknowledged at the time as having a more intellectual society than most other towns of its size in Scotland during this period. There were many who did a great deal to support and encourage Burns' talent and he in his turn supported new developments in the Arts such as the opening of a new theatre in September 1792. The theatre celebrated its bi-centennial in 1992 and remains as the oldest working theatre in Scotland.

Suitably cultural surroundings for the Bard? Yes, but unfortunately there were other aspects of the town's social life which Burns also found congenial *John Barleycorn*, to use Burns' own metaphor, had an established place as in so many country towns of the age. While Burns could be found one evening in refined company at elegant houses with stimulating society, such as that enjoyed at Goldielea or Friar's Carse, he could just as easily be found talking and carousing the night away at the Globe Tavern.

It was not only drinking which lured Burns into trouble, his political views had the same effect. Burns, unlike most of his fellow townsmen, did not condemn the French Revolution which was raging. An incident in relation to the opening of a new public library shows how imprudent Burns, who after all was a Government officer, could be.

Burns had been involved in the setting up of the library and he had presented four books to it. On one of them 'De Lolme on the British Constitution' he had inscribed the words:-

"Mr Burns presents this book to the library and begs that they will take it as a creed of British liberty till they find a better."   *R.B.*

Having had a night to think about the wisdom of these words, Burns rose early and went to where the books had been left. There he pasted the flyleaf to the back of the engraving so covering up his indiscretion - unless it was held up to the light!

In another incident Burns was involved in capturing a smuggling vessel in a particularly bold fashion. The smugglers on board had considerably outnumbered the boarding party. Promotion might well have been forthcoming if Burns had not purchased four of the captured cannon, when they came up for sale, and sent them to France as a gift to the French Convention. Unfortunately the "gift" was intercepted at Dover and an enquiry was ordered into the conduct of Excise Officer Burns. Some biographers have suggested this enquiry blighted all Burns' future prospects. Others suggest he was simply cautioned to be more circumspect in the future. Certainly lively days in Dumfries.

In general Burns' lifestyle in Dumfries was humble but far from poverty stricken. A description of life in Mill Street given by Burns' eldest son suggests a comfortable existence. The parlour and two bedrooms were well furnished and carpeted and there was always a maid.

Burns' days in Dumfries were busy but a long way off from the hard labour of his earlier years on so many unrewarding farms. His excise work, as well as being occasionally lively also consisted of more mundane duties such as stamping leather, checking candle making and licensing transfer of spirits. Sometimes he took his son Robert with him as he made his way, on foot, around the town. He was a noticeable man being five foot ten inches in height, tall indeed for those days.

Later in the day, if the weather was fine, he might be seen on a solitary walk along the Dock Green by the riverside or heading towards the ruins of Lincluden Abbey, no doubt composing lines as he went.

A popular venue in the evening was the High Street where gentlemen would gather to meet the post which arrived around eight o'clock. Discussions arising from the contents of the delivery might well continue in the Globe, for many hours, before Burns returned home. It was after one such evening in January 1796 that Burns lay unconscious for several hours in the freezing cold. Burns did not really fully recover from this unfortunate collapse and his health deteriorated visibly. By March he was described as *gaunt* and by the summer he was lying almost prostrate at Brow Well where he had been recommended to take the medicinal spring water and bathe in the sea. There is no doubt that Burns' health had been badly affected by his early years of heavy work and deprivation. By the age of thirty-seven he was worn out physically and suffering from a recurring heart condition.

The Globe Inn, Dumfries

Burns returned home to Jean, who was expecting another child at any time, and prepared to die. He was under no illusion as to how ill he was. The end came on the twenty first of July.

The Final Resting Place?

As a founder member of the local volunteers Burns' funeral was conducted with military honours. His body was conveyed from the Trades' Hall in the High Street to St. Michaels on Monday 25th July, in the presence of an immense crowd. On the morning of the funeral Jean gave birth to a posthumous son, Maxwell, who died in 1799.

For many years the poet's grave was marked only by a simple slab of stone erected by his widow. Eventually proposals were made to build a mausoleum through public subscription. This was completed in 1815 and took the form of a small Grecian temple. Inside figures of Burns at the plough, watched over by Coila, the Muse of Poetry, were sculpted. Unfortunately there had been no room at the north corner of the churchyard, where Burns was buried, to build the new structure so the mausoleum was built in the south east corner. This meant moving the body.

On 19th September the exhumation was performed largely in privacy. When the vault was opened nineteen years later, to bury the poet's widow, permission was given for a cast of the poet's skull to be made for a phrenological study - we can imagine Burns, if he could have known about this "move" and the skull episode, commenting with wry humour.

Burns' Role in the Present Day

Now we leave Burns in his final resting place and move through the years to Dumfries of 1990's but Burns will simply not be left behind. Although his remains lie safe in his mausoleum Burns' spirit is alive within his writing today. Most would accept that he is more valued now than he was two hundred years ago - his fame is international. In this year of the bi-centennial of his death, visitors will flock to *Burns Country* to visit and savour the places still standing as they did in Burns' day; they will walk the path Burns walked and they will stand to watch the River Nith flowing inexorably to the Solway, just as it did so long ago.

Burns' Mausoleum

"Oh what a canty warld were it,
Would pain and care, and sickness spare it."

Robt Burns

Dumfries has changed but there is still an admiration and dedication to Burns, nurtured by so many local men and women. Just as when the poet was encouraged and supported by local people of vision when he was alive. The wonderful thing is that Burns has not become a myth; a sanitised and unrealistic figure. People celebrate his life for what he was - brilliant, witty, caring, inspired but often imprudent in terms of women and drink. Clearly it was this rich experience of life which made his writing what it is. We read his work and see a man who saw through hypocrisy; who looked at nature; who saw the good and bad in people; who laughed and made others laugh with him and who cried out and wanted others to cry out at injustice and inhumanity.

Many are inspired by their reading of Burns' works and some are inspired to write their own poetry. They too complete an ordinary day's work but then escape into another world where dreams and ideas can be explored. They too can look at odd little incidents or everyday places and bring these alive in images of words and pictures.

Such a family is the Clark family whose work is contained in this book.

John MacDonald Clark was born on the 3rd of June 1914 at Conheath Cottages near Glencaple. The ruins of the cottages still stand. Like Burns before him his parents understood the value of a sound, Scottish education and he attended Dumfries Academy. Those were not the days of students grants, ordinary people, no matter how gifted, seldom attended university. They had to find employment and so John Clark started his working life as a gardener at the Crichton Royal Hospital. He moved on from there to work with the Caledonian Bus Company, first as a conductor, and after his war service, as a driver. His love of words and poetry were always with him and he, with other enthusiasts, established, what may seem an unlikely, company magazine. The *Club Gazette* was edited and contributed to by John Clark but he also submitted articles to a wider audience. He became an active member of Dumfries Writers' Workshop and took great delight in publishing a small book of sonnets *Soul in Orbit* in the mid seventies. A talent with words was matched by a talent as a singer and he enjoyed performing solos at St. Mary's Church, of which he was a lifelong member and long serving elder. The culmination of his writing career in his lifetime came with the publication of an anthology of his war poetry, *Burns' Walk from the Memoried Past* in 1992.

Although a quiet and gentle man he had a keen sense of humour and much of his poetry displays his wit. He could also write movingly of human emotions and evoke strong images of the locality he knew so well. He continued writing in Scots and English right up until his death in August 1995.

John MacDonald Clark's son, also John, was born in Dumfries in 1952. He is a self-taught artist of considerable ability and is well known locally, particularly for his landscapes and watercolours which capture the magic of Dumfries and Galloway. It would have been disappointing if John senior's talent had not been passed on an so it is that in recent years, inspired by his father's work and encouraged by him, John has begun to write his own poetry. Particularly striking are his pieces of landscape poetry produced to compliment an exhibition of his paintings in the Dumfries Arts Festival of

1991. This exhibition successfully launched a series of limited edition prints and many of these evocative works appear in this book.

John combines a demanding career as a financial consultant for a large insurance company with his painting and writing - still finding time to enjoy a happy homelife with his wife and two children.

The final contributor to this book is Alan Clark, grandson of John MacDonald Clark and nephew of John. Alan was born in Dumfries in 1971. Interestingly, photographs belonging to his mother's family suggest that they are descended from Jock Brodie, a well known Dumfries worthy who ran errands for Jean Armour and Robert Burns.

Alan takes us into the technological age being a graduate of St. Andrews University with an honours degree in Computational Science. He has recently been pursuing a career in the computer industry but, like his grandfather and uncle, he has a real talent for words and has been writing poetry from an early age in his spare time.

Now the contributors to this book are all presented - two no longer with us but remembered in their words and two with much still to offer. Two hundred years have elapsed since Burns walked in our town and travelled to other parts of Dumfries and Galloway but this book exists to show that his words still inspire young and old to this very day.

"Here's freedom to them that wad read
Here's freedom to them that would write"

Robt Burns

Sandra M Wilson

The Complete Works of Robert Burns, J A Mackay, Alloway Publishing, Ayr.
Robert Burns, David Daiches, Deutch.
Burns - A study of poems and songs, Thomas Crawford, The Mercat Press, Edinburgh.
A History of Dumfries, William McDowell, Standard Office, Second Edition 1873.

There is a wider space
Above the Earth and Sea,
More beautiful than this world of ours
With all its lakes
Its mountains and its rivers,
And in our quest for self belief,
We overlook sometimes
The hallowed space within ourselves,
The centre of our universe,
The purpose of our being.

J Clark

A SANG O THE NITH

Rin sparklin Nith aye liltin rin
Atween the braes o Enterkin;
Dance whaur the wee winds heid-lang race
Tae glimpse thy bonnie smilin face;
Gar the young mists o mornin spin
Thy maiden goun as fine an thin as ony
lace.

Breathe saftly Nith thy music still
On tree an flooer at Barburgh Mill,
An let thy tremblin imagery
Across thy sleepin bosom play
Fa gently nicht, fa 'neath the hill
Whaur birds, far-hamin, sweetly spill
… their muted lay.

Rest laden Nith by Abbey wa
By storied brig wha's birth ye saw,
For wearied mune an swans maun lean
Like snawflakes on thy velvet sheen:
Rest by this gate ere bolt ye draw,
Here mak thy hame, acclaimed by a
Forever Queen…

J M Clark

BURNS WALK
by the River Nith

Open a gate and leave the town behind,
Sense how the lifted voice,
The traffic's roar die murmuring.
Descend a little lower
And standing on the river's brink
You'll find the trees,
Fresh foliaged and stately,
Lined along one bank.
Now scan the other shore...
Brown earth, green fields rise
In a hedged crazed floor
To mountain walls that meet the sky
And bind the human eye.
A river lies bewitched beneath your feet
The calm depth-saddened pool
Is scarce disturbed,
And there the shallows talk
And strive to reach the far off sea
Enriched by inland quest...
All whispering and cool...
Once balm to him
Who chose this for his walk.

J M Clark

"A down winding Nith I did wander..."

Robert Burns is reputed to have frequented a path on the east banks of the Nith to the north of Dumfries. The route is in fact part of a longer walk of around three miles which stretches from Buccleuch Street Bridge in the town, northwards. This walk can be joined at various places including the Greensands and Nunholm. Burns himself wrote a number of poems praising the river, notably **The Banks of Nith.**

THE COUNTRY KIRK, CAERLAVEROCK

When I get tired o chimneys reekin
An bored tae death wi endless speakin
I whiles can dare
Tae delve beyond mere pleasure-seekin
An yearn for prayer...

'Neath wind stirred trees
Wi leaves upliftin
I'll daunner where the sun comes siftin
An see its kiss
Imprinted on the burn deep driftin
An feel God's bliss...

I'll see the petals o the thorn
Fa shimmerin ower the springin corn;
I'll hear betimes,
My hert athrob this Sabbath morn,
The auld kirk chimes
Wi calm insistence thrill me through,
An fill my mind wi something new...
Nae passin whim
Will bid me occupy a pew
Tae worship him...

J M Clark

From the book *Burns Walk from the Memoried Past* by J M Clark

THE FIRST SNOWS

The snows that fall first
Are the leaves from the trees
Flaking down, unrehearsed,
In a mad strip-tease.

They clung cosily once
To the elm and the oak;
Now they owe no response
To the parent yoke...

And the living green
Of a warm sun's breath
Is the red - gold sheen
Of a garish death.

Anonymous mass
They will shuffle and wheel
To hide in the grass
When the snows are for real...

J M Clark

WINTER SCENE

How quick to change these colours of the
   open field
Where once the branches and the briars
   were so cleverly concealed
Now with a snowy mantle crisp and white
Each darkened bough, each twisting branch
Cannot escape the blinding light.

Exposed, each stalk, each stop, each
   withered leaf
That sought to hide amongst the birth of
   spring
Now caught red-handed like a thief
With no immediate recourse
Unless that which the sun's warm rays
   might bring.

J Clark

"Cauld blaws the wind frae East tae West
The drift is driving sairly;
Sae loud and shrill's I hear the blast
I'm sure it's Winter fairly".

CAERLAVEROCK SCHOOL, GLENCAPLE

Today, the parish name Caerlaverock is associated chiefly with the nature reserve that embraces the Nith estuary. In past times however, it was widely known as a castle of strategic importance. Being border country, the lands and the castle were laid seige to on numerous occasions and were variously in the hands of the English and the Scots. It has been recorded that the likes of William Wallace and Mary, Queen of Scots spent time within its walls. The castle is in ruin today, but is still an imposing sight.

CAERLAVEROCK CASTLE

Caerlaverock... oh... Caerlaverock...
Whit stories ye could tell
O days gaun bye
When roon aboot yer ramparts
And yer bluided gates,
Brave knights alang wi peasants fell.
Yours must hae been a fearsome sicht
Tae them wha never knew...
As closin frae a distance,
Yer might an grandeur grew,

Pity the pair fit soldier then...
Lost in the battle's wail
Forced tae spearhead the ficht
Yer michty turrets scale.
Pity the pair defenceless beast
That carried the fearless knight
Intae the sweat an screamin din
O battle at its height
Pity the frightened drummer boy
Or him wha held the banner
Forced tae dee in the smoke an mud
For somebody else's honour.

"As I cam down by yon castle wa."

Rob* Burns

An whit o the Lords that lived within
The michty fortress gates?
Whit o the servants, cooks and maids
Wha helped tae fill their plates?
Whit o the wretched prisoners
Wha's death wiz sure an slow
Chained in the dark tae the cauld sandstane
In the dungeons far below?
An whit o the bonnie flichtsome lass
That stood on the castle stair
Lookin toward the Solway merse
As she combed oot her tumblin hair?
Whit o the dugs the Master kept
When huntin in the wood,
Whit o the hawk in the castle keep
Or the waifs that begged for food?
Aye mony's the tale that could be telt
Richt doon the ages true...
Caerlaverock nae doot ye'll still be here
A thoosan' years frae noo.

J Clark

Caerlaverock Castle
Dumfriesshire

GLENCAPLE QUAY

There in perspective Criffel lies;
There in the lift the sea-gull cries;
There English hills just tint the skies
Beyond the sands,
And here, where tree clad hillocks rise,
Glencaple stands...

Time was your ancient tide-worn pier
Saw each fine ship yon far point clear,
Saw eager hands her homeward steer...
Her trip complete,
Bringing the yearned-for face to cheer
The village street.

How swelled the proud boat-builders heart
To see the bowspray sunward dart,
The consummation of his art
Brought to her goal...
Each nail, each rivet was a part
Of his own soul.

No longer now can he awaken
To creaking boom and sail wind-shaken;
The march of time, alas, has taken
Toll from the sea...
That old sea-dog has since forsaken
Glencaple Quay.

High tides still 'neath the low shores thud
Their sea-tang yet
May thrill the blood.
Night closes up the wild rosebud
The sun shows red
Ebbtide reflections on the mud
Of glories dead...

J M Clark

From the book *Burns Walk from the Memoried Past* by J M Clark

GLENCAPLE VILLAGE

Situated between Dumfries and the Nith estuary, the Quay at Glencaple took its first cargo on 1747; Maryland tobacco landed by the ship 'Success'. From then on trade flourished as did the smuggling which was rife at that time. Sadly the Quay's operations began to ebb away with the advent of larger bottomed boats and the commercial difficulties of using the river as a trading lane made the use of the 'Dock' impractical. The 'Quay's' commercial use was revived for a brief spell in the early 1990's by cockle boats but 'overfishing' raised environmental issues, and the sometimes controversial 'trade' has now quietened somewhat along this part of the Solway. Glencaple Quay is now used only very occasionally by boats, but in recent years has gained a reputation as a favourite 'mark' for flounder fishing. There are many fishing stories worth recounting of the 'Quay', none more so than the giant 'sturgeon' which unfortunately, for it, lost its sense of direction and somehow swam up the Nith estuary. A local villager not wanting to miss out on the 'fish of a lifetime!' shot it and with others put it on display in a large hut on the 'Quay' end, charging the princely sum of sixpence to see it, which in the '30's would have been a fair sum.

THE COTTAGE

And by the broken bouldered roadway lies
A heap of stones, an unmeant epitaph
To tell in silent language that once here
A cottage stood. A moss-encrusted path
Leads past the remnant. Honeysuckle trails
Where once a gate swung to the knowing
    touch
Of children laughing as they sought the
    shade
For violets, flow'rs which still in beauty show
Beneath the ageing unkempt damson trees,
Long since unpruned and pale against the
    spruce,
Whose living echoes vibrate to the call
Of shrilling black-birds, and the harmony
Of wild doves sighing from their gloomy
    heights.
While in the burn the pebbles, grey and dry,
Rise from the pools, whose limpid sun-
    probed depths
Thrill to the shivering of insect's wings.

When thorns and undergrowth have hidd'n
    from view
This moss-grown pile, perhaps some town-
    tired clerk
Will see new beauty in the woods and
    flow'rs,
Hear music in the rippling of the burn,
And in the frescoed red-tiled bungalow
Enthrone an age-old dream made real at last
And light his Future from the dying past.

J M Clark
at Shoreside Cottage
Conheath

Across the river from Burn's Walk at the conjoin of the Nith and
its tributary, the Cairn, are the ruined remains of Lincluden
College. The first buildings on the site were those of an Abbey of
the same name, built for Benedictine nuns by Uchtred, Lord of
Galloway in the twelfth century. It was converted into a College
by the Earl of Douglas in the 14th century.

LINCLUDEN COLLEGE

Frae Cluden's college hawthorned wood
Upon the river's bend I've stood
An watched above the water's edge
Thro gorse an bush an broken hedge
Distanced frae the human race
Sweet breath o Summer on my face
Freed for awhile frae stress an strain
An like the lifeblood in my veins
That pulses thro me sure an slow
I've lingered on the river's flow
Reflectin a things bricht an guid
Sharin that peaceful solitude
Transcendent frae anither time
Oh wish... that I could ca it mine
An like the birdsong wild an free
Forever I wid contented be.

J Clark

Lincluden College
Dumfries

INSHA-ALLAH (GOD WILLING)
KINGHOLM QUAY, DUMFRIES

Safe in harbour Insha Allah sits
Tethered to bollard...
Secured by rope and line
Shining like a precious stone
Almost contented
She rests
Raised up on metal girders
Above the mud and silt
Biding her time...
Waiting...
Forever patient
For her master to steer her with the tide
Towards the open sea...
Perhaps to fish
Or just to taste again the salted air
And feel the swell beneath her bows
The purpose of her birth.

J Clark

KINGHOLM QUAY HARBOUR DUMFRIES

Built at the same time and for the same purpose as the quay at Glencaple, the Kingholm Quay lies a mile south of Dumfries. Like its counterpart, trade has ceased for commercial purposes and only acts as a harbour for pleasure craft. Many artists are drawn to the area and quite often can be seen sketching the boats and the surrounding countryside. The old warehouses still exist however and a thriving potato business is run from this area.

Kingholm like Glencaple, would have been a busy quay in Robert Burns' day and when employed as an exciseman it would have been his duty to visit the area quite often. John Macdonald Clark's great grandfather was a ships' carpenter to trade and may well have worked in the area in its heyday.

THE BORE TIDE, RIVER NITH

The Solway has always had a reputation for fast flowing tides and there are also areas of quicksand amongst the vast mudflats at low water. The area provided the famous Scottish novelist Sir Walter Scott, an avid admirer of Burns, with an endless source of inspiration for many of his novels.

The bore tide every thirteen hours or so sweeps up the Nith estuary and when conditions are favourable can create a bar of fast moving water up to three feet high. A feature of the lower reaches of the River Nith are the Haaf-Net fishermen who for generations have fished its waters for the famous *Wild Solway Salmon* which appears as a delicacy in many local restaurants and hotels.

"And the same rapid tide shall whelm
The poet and the song"

Robt Burns

THE BORE TIDE

In the first instance there is a song
Too shrill for us; to the water it belongs,
A call from the Moon to her child the sea
'Come and swim the tides with me.'

The Firth responds with eager breath
Anticipates the pull from the Ocean's birth
And in the estuary, the tideways swell,
'Come and dance with me in the Dale'.

From that second, the scene is set,
Sweeps the silt of the banks into a net
The tumult carries all before
'Who will join the party in the land we
     adore?'

The temptation becomes too much for fish
Crustacea flow in the saline mix
Flooding the flats with a foaming tide
'Who else will come along for the ride?"

Gulls above swoop in delight
An easy feast for the pallet in sight,
They too follow the Moon's long call
'Come with me', says She, 'Have a Ball!'

The frilly skirts of the Bore kick high
Leap in merriment towards the source of its
     life
All around are mimicks of the joy
'See the happiness in the games we employ!'

But all too soon the party's done
Down with a crash when the race is run
For the Bore has faltered upon the Caul
The monstrous brother who was there at
     her fall.

There is nothing that the Moon can do
To resurrect her sprightly tune
Which is washed away by the powerful roar,
'To the sea, boys, once, and for ever more!'

A Clark

THE MAN IN THE BLUE SHIRT

Beside the river
The old man in the blue shirt sits
Alone but for his thoughts
Perhaps of love or youth or war.
The silence
Broken only by the heady breath of spring
Hangs heavy as the scent of cherry blossom.

Unnoticed on the grass a crazy dance of
   shadows
Casts a strange hypnotic spell
Inviting anyone close by
To sit for just a moment
And reflect on life's sweet splendour
Its pleasures and its pain.

                     J Clark

"Once fondly loved and still remembered dear."

Robt Burns

GREENSANDS, RIVER NITH, DUMFRIES

Between the Dumfries Swimming Pool and The Rowing Club lies the Greensands. Not far from here, near Buccleuch Street Bridge, was the site of the old Victorian Steam Baths, now demolished, and a fond and not too distant memory for those who had no washing facilities. A sizable flotilla of rowing boats used to tether in the shadow of the bridge but due to the mindless activity of the twentieth century vandal, sadly they too have disappeared. A regatta is held a short distance further upstream by the Dumfries Rowing Club, attracting competition from all over the country.

GUID NYCHBURRIS CALYPSO

This is the Setterday in June
Dumfries guid-neebors gaither roon
An castin aff their cares and hassle
Become the gentry frae the castle;
For them heroic roles are cast,
As pageantry re-lives the past...

At hauf-past seeven the morn begins
While maids still sport their curlin pins;
A courier arrives, post-haste,
Despatches strapped aroon his waist,
Alerts the Provost (hardly waken)
Wi news that leaves the guid man shaken.
Apparently King Robert (Three)
Has a Royal Charter gaun scot-free
An sends it in a palace bag
By messenger on fiery nag.
An ere this restive horse unseats him
Commands that some yin comes an meets
    him.
The Provost in a richt auld fankle,
His chain has slipped doon roon his ankle,
But as he cried aloud: 'That's torn it...'
He spies his Drummer and his Cornet.
'Come, Drummer, wake the populace...
'Noo, Cornet, get your men an race
Tae meet this Royal Charter chiel
While the medieval bell I peel...
Wait, Cornet! At the King's behest
Hear ye his Majesty's request,
(For truth far stranger than fib)
In deference tae Women's Lib.
He noo decrees it's come tae pass
That there should be a Cornet's Lass
Already named for grace an beauty.
Tae horse, then Cornet dae your duty...
I'll wait for you wi a the people
Within the shadow o the Steeple...'

Syne, while they wait wi chat an garble,
Rab Burns looks cool in whitest marble;
There, he sits on his tree-stump,
He maybe glimpses, past the hump
The Globe Inn sign stir in the breeze
An wake his lang-deid memories –
Convivial nights wi cronies spent,

Their tongues wag-waggin, elbows bent;
Or, on a windae-pane inscribin
A verse or twa between imbibin
Across the street anither bounty:
Prince Charlie's sojourn at the County...
Dumfries records that grey December
As no a visit tae remember
He stole their cash by fraud an ruse
Besides a thoosan pair o shoes.
(In vain a wee bird chirped tweet-tweet
Hey, Charlie, they are a left feet;
Your troops, bedraggled, in disorder
Shall limp it hamewards ower the Border)...
While history wails its facts frae myth
The Queen glides radiant doon the Nith
By Royal Barge, thus naethin lessens
Her dignity, her queenly presence,
Her maids o honour, coyly sweet,
Provide a complement complete.
As tae the Steeple they are borne
The sun glows birch as gowden corn;
A sweet voice soars abune the press:
'Queen of the South, thy loveliness...'

As heidin Firthwards seagulls spill
The sun dips low on Corberry Hill,
Then, led by pipers, drums an bands,
A lang procession floods Whitesands;
A cavalcade o' floats an lorries
Frae villages, frae glens an corries
Act oot their fantasy an jest
Wi verve, wi vigour, withoot rest...
Lang efter that, in solemn beat,
Mass bands conjoin tae soond 'retreat';
But, ere black darkness steals the scene,
Fireworks erupt abune Millgreen,
The sky, till noo, a threatenin livid
Is instant magic, sparklin, vivid...
At last subsides the fun, the din,
The Brig-en's blotted oot the mune,
Guid-neebors pairs, but tryst tae meet
Weel-satisfied... despite sair feet...

J M Clark

"...and drouthy neebors, neebors meet."

ROSEFIELD MILLS

Whaur is the chimney
O lang by days
Giant monolith that aince stood guard
Noo draws oor gaze nae mair.

The auld mill stauns its lane
Stane upon hand hewn quarried stane
Mirrored in warm reflection
By the fond remembered kiss
O Nith beyond...

Hoo fared yon chimney stack...
Its final die was cast
By man made cruel blast
Remote controlled.

Yet nane wad witness its sad demise
Or exit frae oor Border skies...
For ere that towerin bulk could fold
A freakish mist arose o mustard hue

An blanketed yon shamefu end
Frae human view...
Thus Nature her ain veil did draw
Owre sic apocalyptic fa...

                           J Clark / J M Clark

"At kirk or market, mill or smiddie..."

Robt Burns

ROSEFIELD MILLS, FROM DOCKHEAD, DUMFRIES.

In 1985 the local authorities ran a competition, the winner of which would have the privilege of detonating the explosives wired to demolish the large industrial chimney stack at Rosefield Mills Dumfries. The young winner was duly announced by the local press and was, no doubt, greatly excited at the prospect of blowing to pieces a monolithic reminder of what was once a thriving industry. And so the stage was set and a sizeable crowd gathered to watch another landmark disappear forever from the Dumfries skyline. Ironically on the very day the event was to take place a strange mist swept up the Nith engulfing the river and the old mill beyond, obscuring from view the very spectacle everyone had come to witness... And so 'Nature her ain veil did draw'...

SHAKESPEARE STREET, DUMFRIES

So named because of the theatre which sits upon it. The Theatre Royal first opened its doors on 29th September 1792 and among its patrons was a certain Robert Burns. The theatre, now the home of an amateur company, was recently renovated, and is the oldest working theatre in Scotland.

A TREE AMONG THE RUINS OF SHAKESPEARE STREET

Destruction's hammers cease; the
   ling'ring dust
Sleeps fitfully along the pitted crust
Of this old street, unwanted now, condemned
To kiss the lowly earth from which it
   stemmed.
Now, gradually, as noise to silence yields,
The after-glow of day from distant fields
Of primrose sky weaves round that weary face
And lines of agony a web of grace.
Too soon it dies, as dies the poet's soul
Craving the stars, but chained to earthly
   goal...
Above the ruins, etched in bold relief,
A single tree, gold laced in every leaf,
Upholds the fleeting torch as who should say:
"'Tis fifty years I've waited for this day..."
Purged, by divine mischance, from filth and
   grease
The long-spurned canvas proves a
   masterpiece.

J M Clark

"AND SPRING RETURNING..."

Though the hills are kissed
Through o reek o mist
By the sun's first warmin glent;
Though tree-shadows rin
Gey sere an thin
Ower the winter-naked bent;
Though the fields are lost
In a jewelled frost,
An the wee snell winds lament,
'Gin a lane bird sings
Oh, what hope it brings
Tae the hert that's winter kent...

J M Clark

From the book *Burns Walk from the Memoried Past* by J M Clark

"While briars an' woodbines budding green."

Robt Burns

CAULBACK DUMFRIES

Caulback... Caulback...
I've looked intae yer waters, deep an dark,
An mony juist like me that ken ye weel
Can ne'er deny they've been enchanted by
  yer spell;
Yer dancin surf aft-times upheld by
Tidal flow... as currents oscillate
Tae clean the san'stane slabs an shingle
Upgaithered frae the river bed below...
Whaur ghaists o simple souls maun sleep
Enticed intae yer cauld embrace where,
Left by fools, were hidden dangers
Nane could e'er forsee...
The grief an sadness o these moments last
Entombed forever in yer timeless past...

Caulback... Caulback...
I've watched an listened
Tae yer ever changin mood...
As 'neath the shadow o the brig ye brood...
A restless spirit that aye spans the Nith
Frae side tae side wi ilk incoming tide;
Yer very nature chainges... Men nae doot,
Great men adoon the storied ages past
Hae marvelled seein ye in frichtsome spate:
Ferocious waters aye an storied calm...
Could be the image in the exile's mind
As memory cairts him back tae auld
  Dumfries.

Caulback... Caulback...

                    J Clark / J M Clark

The Caulback or Caul ranks prominently as one of the major tourist attractions of Dumfries and Galloway. Its tumbling waters swell dramtically during heavy rain which, if pushed back by a rising tide, can cause severe flooding on the Whitesands area of the town. Many shops carry quite dramatic pictures of some of the famous floods that have occurred over the last century. The 'Caulback' built to power the old mill which now houses the famous 'Burns' Centre' on Millgreen is a focal point for visitors from all over the globe and a tourist information centre can be found nearby. Plans are already in place to build a brand new tourist information centre close to the Royal Bank of Scotland not far from Robert Burns' first

CAULBACK RIVER NITH DUMFRIES

house in Bank Street or 'The Wee Vennel' as it was called in Burns' day. This should be completed in 1996. A popular bathing spot in years gone by, tragic accidents in recent times have resulted in bathing restrictions around the deceptively deep salmon pools.

An abundance of birdlife is evident everywhere around this part of the river, no doubt attracted by the endless supply of titbits proffered by locals and tourists. A pair of mute swans build their nest every year in the shadow of Devorgilla Bridge. Their offspring, sometimes seven to eight signets, enthrall locals and visitors alike.

WHITESANDS DUMFRIES

The old burning ground for witches is situated on the eastern shore of the Nith. Its upper portion has long been used as a bus stance for travelling to and from the local towns and villages. Looking across the river above the Millgreen deerpark, it is possible to see the town museum (lit up spectacularly at night). Originally built as a windmill in 1798, it was acquired by the Dumfries and Maxwelltown Astronomical Society in 1835 and houses one of the country's few working camera obscura. Who amongst the astronomical fraternity in those far off days, would have thought in their wildest dreams, that a man with 'Border Blood' in his veins would be first to walk on the moon? Neil Armstrong, a descendent of Johnie, the notorious 17th century reiver, was not only the first on the moon he was also the first man to be made a freeman of the Border town of Langholm in 1972. An interesting analogy which for some years to come made Langholm **the place** to visit for American tourists searching for their Scottish roots. The old windmill or Observatory as it came to be called eventually evolved into a fascinating museum of local artefacts and the impressive building was taken over by the burgh in 1934.

Up until recently the Whitesands played host to one of the biggest livestock markets in the South West of Scotland. Trading mostly in beef and lamb, the farming community would converge on the 'Sands' on 'Market Wednesdays' but due to traffic congestion the markets have been moved to quieter locations in the town. 'Sunday Market' traders have now taken over the areas once covered by sheep and cattle pens, and provide a colourful backdrop with their stalls, selling a wide variety of goods and local produce. At the entrance to one of the markets, a small monument marks the spot where John Kirko, a Convenanter, was shot as a martyr on 13th May, 1685.

WHITESANDS 'BUS STANCE ON A SATURDAY NIGHT (circa 1933)

When ilka licht's a golden chain
Across the Nith's dark pall,
As she spins lippin fu wi rain
Tae clatter ower the Caul.

The mune looks like anither lamp
Abune the auld brig-en;
The pavements shine wi frost an damp -
It's strikin half past ten.

Oh magic 'oor! Oh happy sicht!;
Yon lad halts in his stride
Tae bid his lass a last guid-nicht
An see her safe inside.

But ere he leaves he canna think
Tae pairt juist there an then,
An sae he lingers on the brink;
Sic is the way o men.

At last his fond fareweels are spent,
Then frae his sicht she slips;
He heaves a sigh o deep content,
An starts his fish an chips.

Noo here's a group wi low bent heid,
A sad lang-featured host;
Calamity is theirs indeed -
The 'Queens' hae gane an lost.

There's still tae come the very worst,
Guid reason for sic stoopin,
For presently ane groans: "It's burst!"
An hauds aloft his coupon...

Meanwhile far up the Vennel brae,
Frae ilka airt increased,
The crood, fresh lowsed frae dance an play
Comes linkin six abreist.

Like human sea they flood the Sands
A eager tae discuss
The singers, actors, or the bands
An loath tae seek their bus.

Eleeven o'clock comes chappin oot
The buses manned an syne,
Each in rotation turns aboot tae follow up in
    line...

"Lochmaben", "Sanquhar", and "Carlisle"
Turn eastwards frae the rest;
"Dalbeattie", "Castle Douglas" file
Wi "Moniaive" due west.

An sundry ithers win awa
Till losh the Sands is bare;
I wonder if twas true I saw
A score o buses there.

The lichts are liftin ane by ane,
It's black where aince they showed;
The brig-en's blotted oot the mune -
I'll hirple doon the road.

J M Clark

'While we sit bousing at the nappy
An' getting fou and unco happy
We think na on the lang Scots miles
That lie between us an oor hame.'

Robt Burns

OFF CENTRE MIDSTEEPLE

Yon leanin tower earned Pisa fame
Syne wonder in its people;
An noo Doonhamers feel the same
When gazin at their Steeple.

Sparked off by Nature's weel-worn laws
An fate's eternal twist
This famous, listed landmark has
A measurable 'list'...

Tae politics' prophetic sight-
Glib patter ne'er sae deft-
Proud Tories chant: "It leans right... right!"
Labour intones: "Left... left!".

We cannae boast a tower cock-eyed
As Pisa's storied freak,
But oor ain turret's certified
In yin respect... unique;

For by anither quirk sublime-
Some magical equation-
Midsteeple aye provides the 'time'
As weel's the inclination!!.

                                  J M Clark

MID-STEEPLE, DUMFRIES TOWN CENTRE

Situated at the highest point of Dumfries' High Street, the Mid-Steeple is a decorative building erected at the beginning of the 18th century. Built by the Town Council and now used as a Registrar's Office, its out-buildings are currently retail premises, including a cobblers. It is said that in recent years the building has begun to tilt in the fashion of the tower in the Italian city of Pisa.

MILDAMHEAD MINI-ROUNDABOUT

To ease the traffic flow in Dumfries mini-round-abouts were introduced. The scheme caused much controversy as it was argued that instead of easing traffic congestion they would create potential blackspots. One of the first to be introduced was the mini-round-about at Mildamhead on the Annan Road, conveniently situated near a funeral parlour and chapel of rest.

THE IMMORTAL MERRY-GO-ROUND

The lave weel-versed in three-point turns
Are sweerd tae quote a line o Burns...
Sic treatment o the bard is shabby
By motorists in debt tae Rabbie;
For Lawlands, no tae mention Hielands
Are studded thick wi traffic-islands
Presided ower, time efter time,
By statues o the King o Rhyme.
Aye, while these islands sometimes irk us,
Rab smiles upon oor human circus,
As, nose tae tail, we weave an scoot
Baith in an oot an roon aboot...
If he were in oor midst, indeed
What wad he think o Mildamheid?
Yon mini-Russian-roulette -
Keep lookin richt an place yer bet...
Thus caught up in the endless tide
O motor madness nane can hide...
For them o traffic-sense bereft...?
Co-op funeral parlour's first on left.

J M Clark

DEVORGILLA BRIDGE

Stand upon the bridge
As waters rise in flood
Wash clean its ancient archways
Bound firm by sweat and blood
On this historic crossing
Many a vow was made
Many a heart was broken
Many a trust betrayed.

Look Southwards to the Solway
Where wild geese and whoopers fly
Where ghosts of factories and chimneys
Still etch their presence in the sky.

                                        J Clark

"This monie a year I've stood the flood an tide;
And tho wi crazy eild I'm sair forfairn
I'll be a brig when ye're a shapeless cairn!"

DEVORGILLA BRIDGE, DUMFRIES

Lady Devorgilla was the thirteenth century noblewoman who was mother of the Scottish King, John Balliol. Among her many public works in the area, her wealth provided the first bridge across the river Nith, thus connecting Dumfries with Maxwelltown and Galloway for the first time. The original wooden bridge was later replaced by a stone one which had nine arches. Today, only six arches remain due to work on flood prevention. It was not until the early part of the twentieth century that Maxwelltown finally became part of what is modern day Dumfries.

In hot weather to cool their ardour and impress their girlfriends young men of the town sometimes dive off the 'Brig'. This is not recommended as in Summer water levels can drop to a life threatening level.

SHOE SONG

Twas a boom time for the cobblers
When he came, when he came,
Stole the shoes of boys and men
When he came.

His army was scraped and ragged
As they marched, as they marched,
Looked like frantic, timid rabbits
As they marched.

He took pity on his soldiers
When he saw, when he saw,
But he did us not a favour
When he saw,

That their feet were raw and blistered
Coming through, coming through,
The soles of poor shod slippers
Coming through.

All our boots he demanded
For the King, for the King,
We were walked on by an imposter
For the King.

He left us in the morning,
Heading north, heading north,
Tried to find some safety
Heading north.

When Cumberland overtook them
Beat them down, beat them down,
He scattered the clans apart
Beat them down.

And now our shoes lie rotting
On Culloden, on Culloden,
But the battle's not forgotten,
On Culloden.

A Clark

"The injured Stuart line is gone."

Robt Burns

BONNIE PRINCE CHARLIE IN DUMFRIES

The Jacobite army entered Dumfries during its retreat from England. The force of around four thousand men camped in fields behind what is now St. Michael's Church – where Robert Burns is buried. The Prince himself stayed in the more luxurious surroundings of the County hotel – which has now been converted into a clothes store. It was reported that the Jacobites were rather rough on the locals and stripped them of their shoes for their own wear.

ST. MICHAEL'S CHURCH, DUMFRIES
Robert Burns lies buried in the grounds of St. Michael's Church, interred in a large white marble mausoleum erected in his honour.

GATHERING STORM
(BUCCLEUCH ST. BRIDGE, DUMFRIES)

Fusion of dark clouds threaten this place
And for an instant a state of déjà vu exists
Perhaps from some other life
In Venice's remote canals.

When boats were tethered in another time
Impressing then upon another mind
The weightless image which would hold
Until recalled by some unsuspecting soul
Leaving him in awe and greatly puzzled
Wondering what might have been,
And what might yet would come
In some other daylight dream.

A cold wind blows...
Diffusing any warmth contained
Within the stone and steel...
Of man made structures
Lit by this dazzling sun
Creating this illusion of tranquillity and
    peace
The quiet before the storm.

                                    J Clark

BUCCLEUCH STREET BRIDGE, DUMFRIES

The Buccleuch Street Bridge took three years to build and was completed in 1794 for the grand sum of £4,588.3 - 6d.! It took its name from the Duke of Buccleuch, one of the wealthiest men in Scotland. The Buccleuch estates stretch for many miles across the Scottish border counties. The Duke's home, Drumlanrig Castle, is situated by the village of Thornhill to the north of Dumfries. The castle and its grounds are often open to the public, who not only can enjoy the castle's rooms and treasures but the gardens and an adventure playground as well.

ON ST. MICHAEL'S BRIDGE

I lean athwart the parapet this morn
Ere half the drowsy town
From sleep is torn,
And see the world
As seen through purblind eyes
Beneath the sameness of December skies.
I see the sea-gulls
O'er the river wheeling,
The leaves but lately dead
For refuge feeling... as currents
Bear them past the stirring mill.
The trees show starkly now
Above Craigs Hill –
Black silhouettes against a forge of ashes
Kindling afresh to flame in opal flashes;
Till over Crichton Hill and far beyond
The sky resembles, now the day has dawned,
Myriads of grey geese petrified in motion
Winging across a smoke-shot golden ocean.
But not for long, while lips can hardly dare
To part for breath against the numbing air,
The vision upward melts in flight
Dragging the last pale curtain of the night.
Dumfries, reflected in the Nith's fair stream
Lies all a-quiver in the sun's first gleam.

J M Clark, Dec. 1937

St. Michael's Bridge
Dumfries

ST. MICHAEL'S BRIDGE, DUMFRIES

Opened by the Duke of Buccleuch in January 1927 St.
Michael's Bridge is the most southerly of the town's main four
bridges. Built to ease traffic congestion and provide easier
access to the large industrial textile mills of Nithsdale and
Rosefield its construction was delayed somewhat by the
outbreak of the First World War.

EVENING EPILOGUE

Where Nith at ebb-tide seeks tae win
In hameward flicht the parent Firth
I watched yestreen the shadows rin
Lang efter day had shed its mirth,
An aye, as doon the hills they strayed,
The caller air aroun me played.

Sae tenderly the tide was brushed
That scarce a ripple touched the shore,
A steerin tide, awake but hushed -
A gentle glidin thief she wore
Heaven's goun o blue, an for a crest
The grey-green pallor o the west.

Syne, 'neath lane Criffel's faded hue
The tree-clad fuit-hills mirker turned,
Aloft a star in wonder grew,
Anon anither softly burned...
Instil within me Lord I pray
The peace that merges nicht wi day...

J M Clark

"The Thames flows proudly to the sea,
Where royal cities stately stand;
But sweeter flows the Nith to me,
Where 'Cummins' ance had high command."

Robt Burns

From the book *Burns Walk from the Memoried Past* by J M Clark

'Cummins' is a reference to the Red Comyn slain by Robert The Bruce at Greyfriars Church Dumfries in the 13th century.

RIVER NITH (Near Kingholm Quay)

After passing through Dumfries, the river Nith travels a further seven miles to its estuary on the Solway Firth. The hill, Criffel, dominates the western skyline and among the mudflats and sands of the river mouth live many native and migratory birds. Due to the rarity of some of these birds much of the eastern portion of the estuary was designated part of the Caerlaverock Nature Reserve, which is controlled by the National Nature Conservancy. The reserve attracts ornithologists and nature lovers from all over the world who come to view the wide variety of wildfowl, especially the sometimes spectacular flocks of wild geese, that feed in their thousands, on the rich grasslands and merse of the Solway shoreline.

NOTE ON THE 'BALLAD OF WULLIE WALKER'

Dumfries and Galloway has always been rich in characters and 'worthies' not only in ages past but also in more recent times. Wullie Walker of the poem achieved albeit brief but nevertheless national recognition in the 'Press' when his remarkable record of only issuing five parking tickets in sixteen years of service elevated him to the unique position of 'Best Liked Traffic Warden in the South West of Scotland.'

**THE BALLAD OF WULLIE WALKER
(EX. TRAFFIC WARDEN.)**

He helped maintain a fragile peace
In traffic-conscious Dumfries.
Tae the motor-public Wullie Walker
Became a weel-kent jovial cracker,
Enshrined for them, as patron saint,
In luminous expensive paint;
For durin a his sixteen years
This traffic warden spared their tears
Tae sic a genial extent
He gained wide-spread acknowledgement.

Aye! writers in the national press
Hailed Wull the warden wha'd stuck less
On windscreens o them lethal stickers:
Result? Nae fines or twisted knickers.
Thus countless motorists, 'unfined',
Hae christened Wullie: Wull the Kind,
Amazed at hoo he could contrive
Tae keep his score at lowly: 'Five'...

J M Clark

MOFFAT

The busy town of Moffat itself is a popular destination for tourists who come to enjoy its many walks and parks. During the summer months the population is increased dramatically by visitors and the town is a well known stop-over for bus excursions from all over the country. The many fine hotels which line the main street pay homage to a time when Moffat was famous as a health resort of some standing at the turn of the 18th century. Its popular Physic Wells, a short distance from the town, were a major attraction in their heyday, and many people from all walks of life were drawn to sample the healing properties of its curative waters. In the months leading up to his death Robert Burns was drawn to similar springs at Brow Well in a desperate measure to cure his rheumatic fever. At a time when penicillin was unavailable, his good friend Dr. Maxwell's advice to bathe in the freezing waters of the Solway, combined with energetic horseriding, would today have given good cause for a mammoth law suit and justification for being struck off the medical register.

GREY MARE'S TAIL

A waterfall of some 200 feet, the Grey Mare's Tail is situated on the slopes of White Coombe whose summit is 2696 feet above sea level. The waterfall is located on the A708 between Moffat and Selkirk and the land around it is owned by the National Trust for Scotland. This is a popular destination for tourists and many people enjoy walking on the surrounding hills.

GREY MARE'S TAIL

Shrouded in mist…
Spouting from dark earth
The force of life comes gushing.
Beckoning the spirit and the mind
To drink in celebration,
For here is the ethereal epitome
Of beauty and wilderness combined,
More powerful than human thought,
Created by a deity
As a yardstick for mankind
In knowledge that his endeavours
Will always be amorphous
And humble in design.

J Clark

"At length his lonely cot appears in view
Beneath the shelter of an aged tree;" Robt Burns

CONHEATH COTTAGES (GLENCAPLE)

They've boarded up yon windaes at
    Conheath...
The cottages whaur aince my summers were
Staun silently ower-grown by rampant weeds.
A hopeless vision in their disrepair –
Still obstinate against the freezin gale
Wha's eerie howl backs up the spirits' wail:
Nature's lament arisin frae the airt
Whaur aince was laughter, joy, whar aince
Oor happy childhood holidays were spent
Watchin 'Haaf-netters' bring ashore their
    catch
O siller trophies frae the pulsin tide...
Seein my graun-dad smoke his time-worn
    pipe
Aside the log-fire flickerin in the grate –
When he wad reminisce o lang-bye days
That ships wad tether at Glencaple Quay
Aff-loadin herrin tae the merchants there,
An pey the villagers a shillin fee
Tae supplement their meagre wage-uplift...

The tree still stauns ootside the windae where
My late loved Auntie Martha used tae sit
An paint wi skill the sinkin bluid-red sun –
The sun-set that wad lull the warld tae sleep
Until anither lazy dawn wad stir
The geese an fowl on distant shore ayont.
The tidal Nith wad wake us frae oor sleep
Tae gaze thro misty gless at Criffel there:
A challengin adventure – Braw new day...

J M Clark / J Clark, 1995

Note: J M Clark was born at
Conheath Cottages on 3rd July, 1914.

ON PORTPATRICK CLIFFS

I have stood with my feet in bond
Upon the grey cliffs' utmost edge
Startled to find, unscarred by hedge,
The sea's quiet thoroughfare beyond...
Across a harvest of foam-founded spires,
White-haloed with the circling wings
Of restless gulls it upward flings
The breathing softness
Of a thousand choirs...

J M Clark

*J M Clark pictured at Conheath Cottages just
before the outbreak of the Second World War.*

ROUTIN BRIG
(Near Irongray Church Dumfries)

A place of extreme natural beauty the Routin Brig spans the
Cairn Linn in dramatic fashion creating a vista of rocks and
tumbling water which after a heavy fall of rain literally takes the
breath away. The bridge is bathed in superstitions, one of the
most common being that it is haunted by the spirit of a young
woman in a dark cowl. Her spirit is supposed to haunt the right
hand bank downstream as a contrition for throwing her
unwanted baby from the bridge. A strange rock formation also
exists under the arch of the bridge which resembles a female
form.

ROUTIN BRIG

Braithless stood I ayont the brig
Watchin white waters fa
Owre rock, owre moss, owre stick an fern
Tae shallows far awa.

This neuk o beauty lang removed
Frae busy road or toon
Sang wi a rush o gurglin stream
Aye tumblin doon an doon.

Then instantly my hert upsurged,
Attuned tae music's score,
I kenned fine weel I'd come again
Whaur I'd ne'er been afore...

Aye, here by this sweet linn I'd pause
Tae sample Nature's creed
Breathe deep its wonderment... its peace
Balm tae my soul indeed.

J Clark / J M Clark

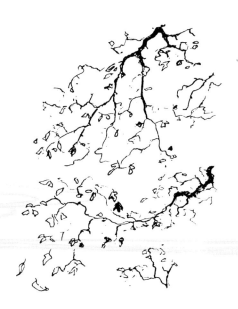

From the book *Burns Walk from the Memoried Past* by J M Clark

THOUGHTS NOT SPOKEN

A distant-sounding gate and footsteps dying
Into a heart-deep silence, busy thoughts not
    spoken...
And still the lazy quiet of shadows lying
A-down the river and beneath trees
    unbroken...
And while for us Time pulses madly on
The tired reflections usher in a swan
So slowly moving that it seems
To bear the tide along
Like music gliding with the burden of a
    song...
For them: the swan, the sleeping trees, the
    tide
There is no Time, no speeding hours exist,
To meet, to be together, to have kissed
Foretells no parting.
'Tis we who turn aside
With sighing half-remembered dreams...

                   J M Clark

Thoughts Not Spoken and **Could You But Know** taken from the book *Burns Walk From The Memoried Past* by J M Clark.

COULD YOU BUT KNOW
(THOUGHTS ON FIRST LOVE)

Could you but sense the power that bids me
   choose
To veil my thoughts in speech lest I should
   lose
     The love I seek to gain,
Or picture my remorse when you depart
Scarce guessing what is buried in my heart,
     Scarce knowing of my pain;
Or were my tongue unloosed as when you
   seem
To wander with me in my every dream
     Or could I soar above
The clouds of doubting, and with a simple
   touch
Release the whisper that would mean so
   much,
     Then would you know my love.

               J M Clark

"Had we never lov'd sae kindly –
Had we never lov'd sae blindly –"

Robt Burns

NOTE ON 'LAY OF THE LAST BUSMAN'

Although John Macdonald Clark never steered a plough as Burns did for a significant part of his life, he did steer a bus for the best part of 38 years. Working as an employee for the old Caledonian and Western bus companies he wrote countless humorous articles on the characters that he worked with and life in general 'on the buses'.

The Lay Of The Last Busman shows not only his ability to laugh at himself but also the quiet sense of humour that embraced so much of his work.

THE LAY OF THE LAST BUSMAN

1.   I studied hard at school,
And finished under Cupid,
I graduated nobody's fool...
Intelligently stupid.

2.   Here's the report my master signed:
A 'busman born and bred,
He has the 'busman's big behind,
The 'busman's tiny head...

3.   So what? The brain at manhood weighs
Three pounds our doctors state,
Thus if you walk round in a daze
You're carrying dead-weight.

4.   A 'busman must, these days of thrift,
A gallon bladder sport
So he may work an OMO shift
And not be taken short...

5.   My jacket is last year's,
My cap's a '68,
My overcoat appears
To bear an earlier date,

6.   But never, ever old
Is my love for you,
You'll never find me cold...
My trousers are split-new.

7.   These trousers are great stuff,
A length of sterling Scotch
With a slender, modern style enough,
But murder at the crotch...

8.   The grim, metallic clank one hears
As I depress the pedals
Is not the chain of former years
But rows of safety medals...

9.   When in the destined plan
I get my final packet
I'll make an exit like a man
Wearing my summer jacket.

P.S. All I ask to kill the time
Far from the daily drama,
Is a grandfather clock with a quarter's chime...
Plus an ugly, seven-pound hammer.

J M Clark

OMO is an abbreviation for one man operation.

TAE A DITHERER

It's easy man, I hear ye yet,
Tae sit cocooned in retrospect...
An' ponder on, aye, haw an hum
On a the things ye could hae done.
Tae mak believe if things could change,
In hindsight hoo ye'd re-arrange
The wrang decisions that ye've made
The foolish things in haste ye've said.
Hoo easy noo it is tae speak
An insincerely friendship seek
An offer whither right or wrang
The handshake that wiz aince withdrawn.
It's easier tae reconcile
The moanin o a simple child
Than understand in life's great span,
The ditherin complexities o man.

J Clark

ODE TAE THE MIDGE

Ponder wi me awhile these michty animals
Which share oor lives as ony welcome cat or
    dog may dwell

In oor gairdens they abide
A million minions, like a pestilent tide.

Say, midgie, what can Ah mak o thee
Wherein lies the purpose that permits ye tae
    be?

Some pests are they that dance at dusk
Aroun oor trees, oor gairden huts.
May Ah ask o them noo, whit are their
    desires
As they hover contented throughoot this
    hour.

Blood thirsty beastie!
Vampirous villian!
Agitatin aphid!
Thrice Ah name thee!

Yet when Ah gaze upon yon specks at this
    distance
Can Ah see the grace in what they are.
Fleein the loop, spinnin and spirallin,
Frolickin lazily, scuttlin, skimmin,
There is mair in their flicht than a pilot and
    plane

Mair than a meagre mote o dust in the air
Sic control is a wondrous complex affair!

Sae Ah admire ye little limpets
Even when ye construe tae pain me
Sae noo let me observe
As ye entertain me.

                                A Clark

"By a theivish midge they had been nearly lost."

Robt Burns

THE DEVIL'S BEEFTUB

In pallor falls the sunlight
In this glen
When the air is wet
And the clouds descend
In this wan light stand I to see
The Devil dancing his cattle
In front of me.

The road from the south
Winds ever up
Until it strikes the heights
Of this sheer cup
There too often for naturally
Roll mists around that Bowl
Of Dishonesty.

I can see in this grim place
The ideal hide
For men of ill repute
To stow their prize
From here God's souls would steer away
Far better to heed their lives
Than to risk the Devil's play.

A Clark

DALVEEN PASS

Leaving your battlements in buoyant mood
I've waded through the heather
On your cheek, and upwards looking
Toward each blunted peak, seen mists
Behind their ragged mantles brood;
Then with the rain I've watched
A milk white flood
Bruising its narrow channel
Headlong seek your rock strewn floor.
I've seen a lessening streak
Of sad, belated snow that has withstood
The wind and rain in shadow
Which the sun has never sought.
And in the night I've heard the wind
Howl free across the moors above.
I've watched beyond the hills
For textures spun
From westward moving dusk
And light deferred
Fanned by the soft caress
Of Nature's love...

J M Clark

From the book *Burns Walk from the Memoried Past* by J M Clark

A FERMER'S BOY FOR TEN MINUTES

Since Tam had been aboot sae high
Until his final term
He'd wished tae doff the auld schule tie
An work doon on a ferm.
He liked the plooman's rollin gate;
His hob-nailed boots as weel.
Noo things aye come tae them that wait
An syne Tam left the schule.
He was a lad wi shoulders square,
A muckle hefty youth;
Sae tae the Dumfries hirin fair
He gaed wi strae in mooth.
An on the road he dreamed his pairt;
Hoo he wad guide the ploo,
Or sit high on the joltin cairt,
Or kep the breengin coo;
An hoo they wad be pleased at hame
Tae learn he was admired...
A Penpont fermer took his name,
An he was duly hired.
He sorted oot his kit that nicht;
His shirts an knitted socks,
An overalls forbye - packed tight
Inside a wee tin box.
An he was oot at break o day
When maist fowk are abed;
His clogs made snug wi whisps o strae;
His hair weel soaked an shed.
A gentle breeze caressed his face
A lark sang in the sky,
As he drew nearer tae his place;
He reached it by an by.
The cobbled close, the white-washed wa's
Fair took his braith wi joy,
An ilka fresh sicht gar'd him pause;
This new-made fermer's boy.
Ere novelty had wearied him
Or he began to tire
A barra laden tae the brim
Emerged frae ben the byre.
Tam keekit ower the midden dyke
Tae see wha steered the shafts;
It was a lass; Tam wavered like
A feather 'twixt twa drafts.
For he had heard o darin deeds
When Kings were crowned at Scone,
An hoo brave Bruce had skelped the heids
O Comyns an de Boune;
Hoo Arthur's knights in mony a ploy

Saved maidens in distress
Tam thocht that as a fermer's boy
He couldna dae much less.
An though the dyke was high an wide
Oot ower it like the wind
He louped an landed at her side;
The lassie stopped an grinned;
An then she laughed; this rattled Tam
As though he had been chidden
He gripped hard each barra tram,
An started towards the midden.
Then up the plank he creaked an swayed
Wi mony a sinkin feeling,
Cursin the day he'd ever made
A bid tae leave his schuling.
But still he sweated tae the trap;
Nae thocht o base retreat;
Triumphantly, withoot mishap
He kept upon his feet.
Noo efter bein led a dance,
Encouragement was needed;
He slung a backward, spierin glance
Tae show he had succeeded.
The lassie clapped her hands a wee
An smirked an said, "Good show",
Tam tipped the barra up wi glee,
Forgetting tae leave go.
An as the lassie won awa
Tae get the coo-hoose cleared,
She heard a splash, she turned an saw
That Tam had disappeared.
Some early workmen heard her din
An asked what 'twas aboot.
She showed the spot where Tam gaed in
An said tae fish him oot.
They rescued him at lang an last;
A great lang smellin lump,
Then tae a rope they made him fast
An hauled him tae the pump.
When finally they'd scrubbed him clean
An Tam kent richt frae wrang
He swore tae them that he had been
A fermer's lad ower lang.

                                    J M Clark

'Oh gie me the lass with the weel stockit ferms!'

Robt Burns

THE MEMORIAL WINDOW TO SIR JAMES ANDERSON, ST MARY'S CHURCH

C Consider how the quality of life
O On this old planet, home of love and strife,
M Must owe a debt to those brave pioneers,
M Marine explorers casting out vague fears,
U Undaunted by unfathomable seas
N Not least the heroes hailing from Dumfries.
I In this proud context burgh history names
C Communications' gallant knight Sir James,
A Atlantic cable-layer aboard his 'iron-clad'
T The fabulous 'Great Eastern' known to every lad...
I In tribute there's a shrine... a picture drawn
O Of window-art – the Bible's early dawn...
N Nominated clearly underneath
S Sir James – a well-earned laurel wreath.

J M Clark

St Mary's Church, Dumfries

A FIELD-MOUSE HAS A FIELD-DAY

The Pooer abune wha did create us
Awarded us an equal status;
But man, big-heided maun deflate us,
    Thro his device
We occupy a wee hiatus
    That's labelled: Mice.

Time was a bard, abune the crowd,
Took up his pen an did us proud;
He visualised beyond this shroud
    O mortal clay
Immortal mice, syne mused aloud...
    Philosophy.

That image didna staun the test;
For us the best was less than best.
Cheese, bacon-rind wi tears were blessed,
    (Man shed a drappie),
Then, twa-faced, murmured: What a pest!
    An waxed trap-happy...

      J M Clark

"Wee sleekit, cow'rin, tim'rous, beastie,
O, what a panic's in thy breastie!"

      Robt Burns

THE LOCKERBIE AIR DISASTER

On the 21st December, 1988 at 6.25 p.m. Pan Am Flight 103 took off from Heathrow Airport. Thirty five minutes later at a height of 31,000 feet above the sleepy town of Lockerbie in South West Scotland, the Boeing 747 was blown out of the sky by a terrorist bomb. No-one who witnessed the tragedy will ever forget the mayhem of that terrible night nor the horrors that were revealed when dawn finally broke.

From relative obscurity Lockerbie was suddenly the focus of world wide attention as the harsh reality of international terrorism made its mark on the town and its inhabitants. The resilience of its people in the face of a world's press hungry for every detail and their determination to get their town back to normal as soon as possible was much to be admired.

With the passage of time the memory of that awful night will eventually fade, but the heartache of those who lost loved ones will never really die. Perhaps when the perpetrators of that monstrous deed are brought to justice will the ghost of *Maid Of The Seas* will finally be laid to rest. Until that day... 'Whae can truly forget?'

Whyles, ranging like a roarin lion,
For pray a'holes an corners trying;
Whyles, on the strong-wing'd tempest flyin
Tirlin the kirks;
Whyles, in the human bosom pryin,
Unseen thou lurks.

Robt Burns

THE 'MAID O' THE SEAS'

Remember the nicht, whae can forget,
The nicht o the fire an the screamin jet,
When on the back o the cauld nicht breeze,
The deil tore apart... the 'Maid O The Seas'.

Remember the nicht, whae can forget,
The nicht o the fire an the screamin jet,
When death an destruction came thunderin
    doon,
Tae tear at the hert o an innocent toon.

Remember the nicht, whae can forget,
The nicht o the fire an the screamin jet,
The heat an the smoke, an the terrible din,
When metal an brick baith fused intae yin.

Remember the chill o that smoulderin dawn,
An the horrors we saw, as the warld looked
    on,
An the blackened great hole wi its sides grim
    an steep,
That swallowed the lives o them in its keep.

Well they've filled up the crater, tae bury the
    pain...
There's a gairden there noo... a memorial
    stane,
There's flooers an a seat, an they've planted
    some trees,
For them that wiz lost... wi the 'Maid O The
    Seas'.

...Gien the passage o time, they say we'll
    forget,
The nicht o the fire... an the screamin jet?

J Clark

JOHN BRODIE

John Brodie was a well known worthy in Dumfries and as a lad used to run errands for Robert Burns and his good wife Jean Armour. A scalliwag, poacher and a storyteller of note he is often mentioned in historical references to characters of Dumfries. Loosely related to Alan Clark whose poems appear in this book, he lived to the remarkable age of 98 years, which in Burns' day was quite an achievement. Despite his sometimes questionable way of life, he was liked by all who knew him and William M. Taylor, a correspondent of the day, wrote the following poem in his honour.

'A' ye wha live by sowps o' drink,
A' ye wha live by crambo-clink,
A' ye wha live and never think
Come mourn wi' me!

Robt Burns

JOHN BRODIE 1777 ~ 1875

Mourn Dumfriesians ane and a'
Frae Tinwald Hills tae Hoolet Ha',
And ither lands sae far awa
The news will speed
And tell about the sad doonfa,
John Brodie's deid.

The loss o John we deplore,
Nae mair he'll hirple ower the door.
And tell about the days of yore
And mony a scene.
A vennel callant tae the core
Kent Burns and Jean.

An honest hearted social cheil,
A heart that could for ithers feel,
"The gentle art" line, could him learn.
But noo he's bade his last fareweel
Tae Nith and Cairn.

John had mony curious things,
Worm-eat fiddles wantin' strings
And tooth picks in the shape o' tings,
Hung on a nail,
And banties stuffed wi' pented wings
Were a' for sale.

A matchlock o' Prince Charlie's day
That witnessed mony a bluidy frae,
And next his gun he used to say
Made by a foreigner,
Tae shuit, in lands saw far away,
Aroun' a corner.

The bonniest thing I've got, he said,
A basket hilted hielan's blade,
That witnessed mony a border raid
In war and peace,
And owned by Burns, I've heard it said,
In auld Dumfries.

Scotch history was his heart's delicht,
The days o Bruce and Wallace wicht
He'd talk on them the hale lang nicht
The best ere born,
And say there ne'er was sic a fecht
As Bannockburn.

He kent the country far and near,
Frae Criffel tap tae Durisdeer,
And folk that kent him when they hear,
Their hearts will bleed,
And ower his memory drap a tear –
John Brodie's deid.

Wm Taylor, Dumfries May 29th, 1875

THE GREY MARE

The heart was pounding in the galloping
   grey
As it sped up the scree slope
Charged up the brae
For the chase had been issued
And the warnings were grave
The pack were a-hunting and
The mare was the prey...

And so it ran –
Quickly, surely, always truly,
Upwards towards destiny,
Not knowing what was to come:
The mare hating the hunters' run.

It crested the hill and sprang on its way
Muscles acquiver, lungs fired and strained
Pushing and pushing and further again
Yet the pack still were closing
To corner the game.

And then it fell –
Just in that instant that would have sent it
   to Hell
The springing beasts sent sprawling,
The mare tumbling, free falling,
Downwards and downwards through a gully
   that was calling

Out the grey mare's name...
The grey mare...
Grey mare...
Mare...

And still today:
Listen by the hillside
For the story yet remains
In the echoes of the past
In the crag where fierce waters drain.

                   A Clark

DEVIL'S BEEF TUB
(Moffat)

This wealth of rolling hills
To right and left
Once lured the hunted
And inspired the brave...
Now by the roadway
Oe'r a martyr's grave
A monument against a blackened cleft
Stands guard alone.
The upland wind bereft
Of trees and hedges runs
Where wave on wave
Of redd'ning ferns make motley.
Men who gave their souls for plunder,
And were wondrous deft
In ways of torture
Here sat round their fires;
Saw this same mist swathed sunrise
Clean the hills or looking southward,
Scanned the wooded sweep
That all but buries
Moffat's peeping spires...
The moor-fowls cry that woke them
To new ills... now calls the shepherd
But to tend his sheep...

J M Clark

From the book *Burns Walk from the Memoried Past* by J M Clark

DEVIL'S BEEF TUB

On the A701 north of Moffat a natural basin is formed by the opening up of the surrounding hills. The depression was nicknamed the 'Devil's Beef Tub' and it became the hideout of cattle rievers who robbed the drovers of their money and cattle. This practice ceased towards the end of the nineteenth century when the development of the steam engine allowed cattle to be traded far more rapidly and securely between Scotland and England.

SWEETHEART ABBEY

Great archways rise from perfect green
Broken by time into accidental harmony.
Colossal windows,
Re-sculptured by wind and rain,
Now stand free... of glass, of wood, of tile,
Allowing sunshine to wash this hallowed
Place with light...
Cleansing the sandstone portals,
Wrought by human pain...
The pain of grief,
Brought on by love of Balliol...
Long dead.
Entombed within this shrine,
His heart, and hers,
The Lady Devorgilla's...
Forever to remain.

J Clark

"And I will luve thee still, my dear,
Till a' the seas gang dry."

Robt Burns

SWEETHEART ABBEY
(New Abbey A710)

The Abbey was built by Lady Devorgilla in 1275 as a memorial to her late husband, John Balliol. His heart was embalmed by her on his death and was later encased within the walls of the Abbey, which was populated by Cisterian monks. The Gothic splendour of the Abbey can still be seen in the ruins, and its complexity indicates that the building had been erected by people specially imported into the area by Devorgilla for this purpose.

ODE TO THE "FLYING COFFEE POT"

O! Elvanfuit
A queen ye sit!
I've seen your hills an passes day an dark,
Your sheep, an lichtsome lassies – question
   mark.
The bare muirs stretch awa on either side,
An hirplin at your feet the infant Clyde
Transforms your solitude, an brings as weel
A host o fishermen wi rod an creel;
But what brings ye your fame in human annals
Is far removed frae peacefu nature's channels:
An unleased monster daily passes by
An droons wi clangs an shrieks the muir-fouls
   cry.
I thus refer, in case ye canna guess
Tae that wild brute, the Leadhills steam express:
The very mithers lull their weans tae sleep
Wi tales o hoo it raced a drove o sheep,
An hoo that nicht the puir beasts staggered
   hame
Their heids between their feet for very shame.
Hoo oot the lum flew lumps o burning coal
An scorched the heather-bells frae ilka knoll.
Had he was did it for a record's sake
Foreseen the devastation in his wake
He wad hae turned wi fury on the stoker,
    An choked him deid, or blin't him wi the
    poker...
Noo let's be thankfu' that the birds lang syne
Had ceased frae buildin nests alang the line,
Since passengers got doon tae stretch their legs
An came back wi their pockets fu o eggs...
Faith, aye! but for that cruelly stated
The puir birds' gorlins wad hae been cremated.

O, Elvanfuit!, O, Elvanfuit!
Your women knit, men smoke an spit,
An ponder on the terrors o this age,
Wha aince kent only sheep an winter's rage.
Still, noo ye hae thro this same awfu speed
A close proximity tae Wanlockheid!
Castles can boast the seiges they've withstood,
But Wanlockhead can boast its altitude...
Toon chimney-stacks an city spires are braw;
The sma'est cottage here transcends them a.
Then, let us praise the medium that unites
Twa villages on elevated heights.

There micht be ither trains, but they are few
That keep a by-gaun place as lang in view...
They say folk staun for 'oors upon the green
Wavin' their hankies tae a pairtin freen;
I wadna wonder did they no get wise
Tae benefits derived frae exercise,
An, in the years tae come, hae case tae mind
That sawed-off benefactor o mankind...
What chance, then, has the 'Coronation Scot'
In competition wi the 'Coffee Pot'?

J M Clark

VIADUCT AT RISPING CLEUCH
4 MLS FROM ELVANFOOT

"Like racking engines!"

Robt Burns

LOWTHER HILLS

An old Roman road was the principal route which opened up the Dalveen pass from Elvanfoot to Durisdeer through the high lands of the Lowther hills. This pass was improved upon the advent of the modern A702 which connects the A74 to the A76. Further north in the hills sits Scotland's highest village, Wanlockhead. At 1531 feet above sea level it was once a lead mining settlement. The mine shaft is today part of a mining museum. A steam locomotive, nicknamed the 'Coffee Pot' once ran from Wanlockhead to Elvanfoot.

AUTUMN BURNINGS

Let all the rain come down and soak the
land in puddles
In rivulets and hollows
On this leaden day.
For there is a glimmer in the undergrowth
An inkling of hope that a seed will rise forth
Into the majesty of its roots –
Roots to branches and trees, roots to
    ancestors and parents –

Its parents,
Look, can you see them now?
Those who stood once as proud and
    bejewelled as royals:
Scarlet to russet, amber to ochre
Those who were so mighty and strong
Their bare bark a shadow of their lives long
    gone.
Now only their ghosts remain to remind the
    tide of their past fame,
Those who were struck down by an
    autumnal flame.
Look, can you see them now?
Sad sentinels guarding the shore from the
    sea.
Watery wraiths in the rain.
Look, can you see them now?

A Clark

"The yellow autumn presses near."

Robt Burns

ROUGH ISLAND
(Seen from between Rockcliffe and Kippford)

The Jubilee Path as it is called is only one of many coastal walks designed to allow access to the beautiful and sometimes quite dramatic scenery of the South West of Scotland. Blessed with a mild climate in the hot summer months the headlands can become tinder dry and occasionally small bush fires will create strange landscapes. Recovery is quick however and the wild gorse soon recovers along with flowers of every description. At low tide Rough Island can be reached by a causeway although at certain times in the year the public are asked not to disturb the wild birds which use the island as a nesting ground.

A COMPLETE GUIDE TO THORNHILL
27th November, 1937

Tae ye wha wish a lastin thrill
I hereby recommend Thornhill,
Far-famed for sic-like delicacies
As sausages an bonnie lassies.
Anither thing attention begs:
A horse o stane on its hin legs,
Upreared upon a fluted column,
Looks lively whiles, an syne looks solemn;
Tae even further cramp its style,
They've built below a desert isle;
Nae palm trees here, nor trailing vines,
Sole populace, twa "Keep Left" signs,
An whilst the lang airm o the law
Will mak its shores a port o ca.
But doon the street what's sure tae please,
There blooms an avenue of trees;
The cutest tree ye ever saw
Conceals the local cinema.
O public buildin's here on view,
Visit the "George" and the "Buccleuch"
Or that embodiment o licht,
The gas-hoose staunin first on richt.
My purpose hasnae been tae mention

Amenities that force attention;
But ane that merits an ovation
Must surely be the local station:
Even the critics maun be lenient
An sat richt noo that it's convenient,
Or if its no wha then wad grudge
A paltry twa or three miles trudge?
As backward at Thornhill ye raise
Yer een or haun in silent praise,
Ye maun not let yersel forget
The countryside in which it's set;
For had ye wished an artist's feast
An hirpled North instead o East,
Wad ye a thocht it "infra dig"
Tae tak a squint at Carronbrig?
Tho aiblins there's a nobler scene –
Drumlanrig Castle framed in green.
On this same road, an further Sooth,
There bides a rather curious truth;
Each sign-post as it westward faces
Directs ye tae the same twa places.
Perchance ye'll mind the auld decree
That ye man see three toons an dee;
The first o these ye micht survive –
Naples, Penpont, an Moniaive.

J M Clark

SANDYHILLS

Echoes of my childhood linger here
Rocks that once were mountains
Touch a water colour sky
Warm grains of sand like gold dust
Through my fingers slip
Each one a polished stone in miniature
Filtering downwards... sparkling in the sun
Marking time like hourglass beads
Bringing back visions of my youth
When brightly painted buses came in con-
voys
And almost as one emptied hordes of
    laughing children
On to damp and golden shore...

Sandyhills will always be a special place...
Full of memories and dreams.

                                        J Clark

'We twa hae paidl'd in the burn
Frae morning sun till dine;
But seas between us braid hae roar'd
Sin auld lang syne.'

SANDYHILLS BAY
(Near Dalbeattie on the A710)

One of the best and most popular beaches along the Galloway coast, Sandyhills is a favourite with locals as much as with tourists. At low tide, the waters recede to a great distance leaving a vast expanse of clean yellow sand, and when the tide is high, the shallow decline of the bay makes its waters ideal for bathing.

AE VILLAGE
(A701 near Parkgate)

Britain's shortest named village, the Ae (pronounced as in capital 'A') village sits alongside Ae water which in turn runs through Ae forest. This is Forestry Commission owned land and contains several popular public walks.

A PHONE CONVERSATION ABOUT THE AE VILLAGE

'Ae village, by Ae Water in Ae Forest',
That was the address, I said.
The Englishwoman on the phone sounded perplexed,
As if I were soft in the head,
'But what is the address?' she enquired
And I replied with my tongue in my cheek,
'It's the same as that on the form
'Which was sent to you last week!'
She must have looked at it bewildered
For a minutes silence then ensued
And thought I was taking advantage
Of her sassenach's Ps and Qs.
So I repeated the address more slowly
'Ae village', that's what I said
'By Ae water in Ae Forest,
'Go to Lockerbie and head north-west.'
She muttered me a salutation —
A 'Thank you' I think it was
And perhaps it finally dawned
On her that I was being honest
And she was not being conned.

But somehow I doubt it.

A Clark

THE ADMIRABLE CRICHTON

James Crichton, the 'Admirable Crichton', was born at Eliock, Sanquhar on the 19th August 1560, a descendent of King Robert II. Educated at Cluny, Perthshire and St Andrews University he could speak twelve languages and was learned in almost every sphere of contemporary knowledge. He travelled to France and later to Italy to improve his education, but was treacherously killed in Mantua by the jealous son of the Duke, Prince Vincenzo Gonzago on the 3rd July 1582, when he was already renowned as 'Admirable'.

OUR ADMIRABLE CRICHTON

In St Andrews by the Old Diner is a plate
That commemorates a Crichton of
   achievement great
Such an Admirable man was he
So chivalrous in his acts and deeds
That they took a wall to write down his fate.

Now, this worthy was of noble birth
A refined gent; superior turf
Mighty good with his horses
Fluent in language, science and the sports
That previous few round the Burgh could
   have matched his worth.

There is a lesson told here, if you're too good
   by far
For Crichton was supposedly in fencing a
   star.
Not good enough it appears,
Since some less classy peer
Felled our Admirable Crichton with a quick
   thrust spar.

Alas! Poor Crichton was at death's door
Far too adept for this world to adore
And passed out of this life
Departed to Heaven where the Admired are
   rife
Our Admirable Crichton, to death, a bore!

                                    A Clark

KIPPFORD REVISITED

Again I wandered down the old
Road's magic staircase to behold
Anew this first love. There the bay,
A harp of silver water, lay
Between the knees of sleeping screes
This harp, with lazy ripples strung,
Thrilled to the sun,
And round me's sprung
A soundless symphony,
Not played for human ear
But fragments strayed unknown to art
From beauty's heart...
Not here the cauldron's fiery heat,
Or patter of time fretted feet;
Not here the ceaseless pounding wheel,
But paint-pot brush and upturned keel,
And random spar sea-rack and tar;
And houses climbed the granite face
Above the gorse for better place
To see the far hills, distance wreathed,
Where tidal Solway stirred and breathed,
Or Nature pointing, with a friendly nod,
The intricate simplicities of God...

J M Clark

KIPPFORD
(Off A701)

The quiet village of Kippford is an ideal retreat for those who like sailing and walking. The marina boasts a wide variety of boats and a picturesque caravan site provides holiday accommodation. The Anchor and Mariner hotels both offer tempting food with locally caught seafood a speciality. There is a small art community here and the walk leading down to the shore at Rough Island will reveal a few artistic surprises.

NETS AT DOUGLAS HALL

There is a silence here...
A quiet embracing calm.
For when the tide recedes
And leaves behind this vast expanse of sand
There seems to be no threat
No danger... How can there be
Only the salmon nets exist
To cut into the sky
And break that perfect symmetry
Of cool reflected light
On pools and creeks
Stretched... far as the eye can see...
There is no danger here...
How can there be...?

J Clark

DOUGLAS HALL BAY

Nets have been used in the Solway and other parts of Scotland for many generations. Before stake nets became common place it was recorded that in the 16th century fishermen were seen to enter the Nith on horseback and catch fish with a three pronged spear. Although when the tide is out the vast mudflats seem a safe walking ground when the tide sweeps in deep channels fill quickly and can cut off the unwary from the safe reaches of the shore.

SOUTHERNESS POINT, SOLWAY FIRTH

Situated south of Kirkbean the Southerness (Satterness) lighthouse is the oldest along the Galloway coast. During its working life it was used to guide ships through the difficult channels of the Solway Firth; a great deal of trade in those days taking place with Virginia. The remoteness and isolation of the area made its many coves and bays ideal for the smuggling of contraband into the country – a practice often achieved with the compliance of the locals and which gave rise to the area's reputation as the Smugglers' Coast.

SATTERNESS (Southerness Light)

They traversed the channel by your beaming
    eye
When you gazed seaward on the darkest
    nights
And never a glance in anger did you pay
    those men
Whose merchandise brought profit to your
    paymaster's den

So proudly standing on the rocky shore
Boldly taunting the men of the law
Whose poor vigilance along the coast
Was the jibe of many a tavern boast

Satterness... Strong and erect in your
    mischievous youth
Your miscreance your measure of manliness
What if the King's men had learned the
    truth
About the seaman who brought Virginia's
    best

Now the lone stonework stands pale in the
    bay
Like some ancient temple that had
    worshipped the day
You had worshipped the night
Now even your acolytes have taken flight
Satterness... Once Lord of the night.

A Clark

"She shines sae bright to wyle us hame..."

Robt Burns

FADED LEAVES

Dark leaves lie deid upon the moss
Doon by the laden burn;
Bare trees may weel forget the loss
O what can ne'er return;
They ken when Spring hies up the glen
She'll find green blossoms there again.

Loves leaves, though faded, roun me
Cling... They still my hert entwine,
But should they fa there is nae Spring
Can help tae keep them mine...
Oh, lassie will ye see them lie
Withoot a tear, or passin sigh?

J M Clark

'Roving winds around her blowing
Yellow leaves the woodlands strowing'

Robt Burns

From the book *Burns Walk from the Memoried Past* by J M Clark

RESTLESS NIGHT

Cool is the pillow on which I lay my head,
Restless the night,
As I meander through my dreams...
Woken on occasion by shafts of light
As night air through my window
Breathes gently on the blinds,
Silently nocturnal shadows dance
An ancient rhythm, older than time.
Softly I breathe, lest I should wake my love
So tranquil in her sleep,
So sweet the fragrance
From she who shares my bed...
And so the night turns to day.

J Clark

LAST RESTING PLACE

What fearsome foreign tidal rip
Tore her from the mother ship?
Or was she set adrift, unmanned,
Released by foolish, thoughtless hand
To float, without a friend to guide
Controlled by movement of the tide;
Till when on some sad aimless quest
Her broken timbers came to rest,
Bleached by cold and salty air
The fragile hull, beyond repair,
Lay waiting...
Stripped off all dignity and pride...
For that last high incoming tide
To move these poor remains with grace
To this, their final resting place...?

J Clark

The deil's awa, the deil's awa,
The deil's awa with th' Exciseman!
He's danc'd awa, he's danc'd awa,
He's danc'd awa with th' Exciseman!

Robt Burns

CARSETHORN
(Solway Coast)

Once used as a port of Dumfries, the village is located to the north of the Southerness lighthouse on the eastern lip of the Nith estuary. It was a place for excisemen, like Burns, where they could keep watch for smuggling activity in the area. Another famous son of the area, John Paul Jones, born a few miles away at Arbigland, would have been attempting to dodge the excisemen. He later went on to found the United States Navy.

ROCKCLIFFE

Peaceful now as tide recedes
From sand and rocks and weed
Fresh water from a higher ground
Meandering through a granite filter bleeds...
Feeding the sea...
Which soon will all be gone
Exposing an expanse of mud
As far as the eye can see
And for a time at least
The birds can feed on shrimp and worm
Undisturbed... unless by man
Until the tidal forces sweep again
The rushing waters to the land.

J Clark

ROCKCLIFFE
(Off A710 at Colvend)

A short journey south-east from Kippford takes one to the resort of Rockcliffe. Like its neighbour, Rockcliffe is ideal for those who like the quiet ways of life. Perched around the bay on the hillside are numerous expensive villas not too dissimilar to the sort one would expect to find in a village on the French Riviera.

THE CAIRN

Standing
Stones alone
The cairn guides
The wayfarer home
I hope that while I travel
This road... My prayers will
Show me...   The path to go.

A Clark

NIGHTFALL IN THE MABIE FOREST

This may be the last time we see each other,
   love
If we're not quick the dark will hide our way
Then who will guide us on together
Through the trees, the dells and braes?

The owls are waking to their hooting
I can see in shadows creatures move
Now hold me close and let's keep walking
Before we miss our final post.

Although it's a long journey through here
And it seemed so pleasant at the start
The gloom began descending far too quickly
Our path become mired in the dirt.

It's a long walk from the edge of the forest
If ever we miss the home trip's bus
Let's pray that the moonlight assists us
And the directions are clear and robust.

Stay near, may we never be parted,
Be close, and my love, never stray,
I never wanted our love to be thwarted
By a lack of hours in the day.

A Clark

'Wishfully I look and languish
In that bonnie face o' thine
And my heart it stounds wi anguish
Lest my wee thing be na mine'

Rob Burns

CARSETHORN AT DUSK

Out beyond the stones
Washed and weathered, water honed,
That spread first right then left
Across this stretch
Shine the limp lights of Cumbria's homes.

At dusk the clouds descend
To cover the couched dens of the
   Englishmen
And Gloom becomes the shady name
Of the Firth's frothing, foaming mane.
At Carsethorn, as the night deepens.

Standing at the shoaling Solway's side
The embankment sounding to the sucking of
   the tide
I fear the earth's attempts to imbibe on me
A lie that this place could well be
The world at the End of Time:

At Carsethorn, night deepens.

A Clark

RETURN

I never dreamed of this...
That we should walk some cosy lane
Together through the cooling bliss
Of yielding ferns, hearing the rain
Tap-tapping out its magic score above.
I thought such things were o'er forever.
And then I never knew
That sprigs of honey-suckle grew
Profusely sweet among the thorn,
That on each cottage hedge were born
Such roses... the shameless scented red,
Or this one, creamy tinted,
With modest drooping head.

I never thought I'd climb
Halfway to heaven in time to realise
This earthy sun-warmed scene
Beneath our feet was beautiful and clean
I'd never have the lasting memory
Of a kiss, if I had dreamed all this...
Never quite fulfilled
Was Summer's promise; never stilled
The sadness of remembered things...
The happy glance... the first shy kiss,
And all the tender hopes that fall
Leaf upon leaf in slow autumnal dance...
I think we make too much of happiness;
We seek for such with all our yearning,
Failing still to hold in heart's
Captivity the joy that lingers free
As the sun-blest breath...
Stirring your hair to gold...

J M Clark

From the book *Burns Walk from the Memoried Past* by J M Clark

THOUGHTS AT THE GLOAMING

Rest on the shining oar
Watch how the ripples die
Widening from shore to shore,
Catching the amber sky;

Drift with the pulsing tide,
Swing with the breath of wind;
Think when the last bird cried
And the grey gulls dinned.

Hills in your blackness clad
Mourn where the sun has set;
Twilight serene and sad
Can I my love forget?

Point where the stars' first gleam
Deepens the russet hue,
And leave me with the tide to dream
A dream, my love, of you...

J M Clark

From the book *Burns Walk from the Memoried Past* by J M Clark

GOING HOME

Into the darkness of a night-time travelling
   home
Quiet all round me, the thrum of the engine
   drones,
As forward the path unwinds
And I, weary traveller, speed on.

It might as well be space outside
The evening clouded shuns the light,
While I in my cockpit guide
The bulkwark that sustains my life.

And here and now an intruder skates
Passed on the tarmac to another place
His lights a sign of life beyond
Swimming also this river's race.

So slow the miles slip ever past
Time opts to crawl as a means of fast
Never will this journey end
But stretch forever until its last.

I descend into the valley deep,
Plunge into the warm waters, wet my feet
As the sky lights; getting brighter
My destination awaits - Dumfries.

A Clark

"How slow ye move, ye heavy hours."

Robt Burns

TREE

My Papa, my Uncle, my Brother and me,
Are just three generations from my family.
A poet so fine, brings back memories of mine,
On this branch which is part of my tree.
The second branch is picturesque, as pretty as a picture.
This leaf of my tree has been painted.
Along comes the third and here it all rythmes,
The writing revealed in its blossom.
And then comes me, part of my tree,
Drawing it up for all to see.
Along with my tree grows talent,
And talent there always will be.
My Papa, my Uncle, my Brother and me.

TRIBUTE by Sharon Clark

NOTES ON CONTRIBUTERS

JOHN MACDONALD CLARK 1914-1995

John Macdonald Clark was born at Conheath Cottages, Glencaple, near Dumfries on 3rd June, 1914. Educated at Dumfries Academy, he left school to become a gardener at the Crichton Royal Hospital. He moved on from there to work with the old Caledonian Bus Company, formerly as a conductor and latterly, after the Second World War, as a driver. His love of writing led him with others to establish a company magazine called the 'Club Gazette'. Acting both as editor and subscriber he submitted many articles not only to the magazine but to local and national papers of the day. An active member of the Dumfries Writers Workshop many of his witticisms were broadcast via Radio Scotland and a small book of sonnets entitled 'Soul In Orbit' was published in the mid-seventies. A trained singer he was often called on to perform as a soloist by St. Mary's Church where he was a respected elder for many years. An anthology of his war poetry entitled *Burns Walk From The Memoried Past* was published in 1992 and received favourable comment within the Dumfries area. A quiet and gentle man, in his late years he often helped his son John to rework poetry into 'auld Scots' and continued writing humorous poetry right up until his death in August 1995.

JOHN CLARK

John Clark was born in Dumfries in 1952. A self taught artist, he is best known for local landscapes and his watercolours can be found hanging in local galleries and Summer Exhibitions in and around Dumfries. Inspired by his father's work, several pieces of landscape poetry were produced to complement an exhibition of his work held at James Thin as part of the Dumfries Arts Festival in 1991. The exhibition successfully launched a series of limited edition prints, many of which appear in this book. Over the years he has contributed to many mixed exhibitions with prominent local artists and for some years served on the executive council of The Dumfries & Galloway Fine Arts Society. Apart from a brief spell with I.C.I. he has worked for the last 19 years as a financial consultant with the Prudential Assurance Company. Copies of most of the prints which appear in the book are available via James Thin, Church Crescent, Dumfries or by contacting the artist direct on 01387 263280.

ALAN CLARK

Alan Clark was born in Cresswell Maternity Hospital, Dumfries on the 7th March, 1971. Photographs belonging to his mother's family suggest that they are descended from Jock Brodie, a well known Dumfries worthy. Town records indicate that as a boy Brodie ran errands for Jean Armour and Robert Burns. Apart from several months in Lochgilphead, Argyll, Alan's schooling took place in Dumfries, firstly at St. Andrews Primary and later at St. Joseph's College in the town. Sufficient exam results allowed him to continue his education and four years later he emerged from the University of St. Andrews with an honours degree in Computational Science. Over the last two years, work in the computer industry has taken him to York, Essex and latterly Edinburgh. He is a keen sportsman and played for the University football team amongst others. He has been writing stories and poetry from an early age inspired by his late grandfather, John Macdonald Clark.

ROBERT BURNS
POETRY EXTRACTS AND REFERENCES

Page

ii   *"A tender father and gen'rous friend."*
      – 'Epitaph for Robert Aitken Esq.'

xi   *"O'what a (canty) warld were it (cheerful)*
      Would pains and care, and sickness spare it."
      – An address to the Colonel of the Dumfries
      Volunteers.

4   *"A down winding Nith I did wander."*
      – "A down Winding Nith."

8   *"Cauld blaws the wind frae East tae West".*
      –'Up in the Morning Early."

10   *"As I cam down by yon castle wa."*
      – "As I Cam Down By Yon Castle Wa."

18   *"And the same rapid tide shall whelm the poet*
      And the song."
      – Elegy on Stella. A poem transcribed by Burns.

20   *"Once fondly loved and still remembered dear."*
      – "To An Old Sweetheart."

23   *"And drouthy neebors, neebors meet."*
      – 'Tam O' Shanter.'

24   *"At Kirk, market, mill or smiddie..."*
      – 'The Twa Dogs.'

27   *"Whiles briars and woodbines budding green."*
      – Epistle to J. Lapraik.

31   *"While we sit bousing at the nappy"*
      – 'Tam O' Shanter.'

36   *"This monie a year I've stood the flood an tide;"*
      – 'The Brigs O' Ayr.'

38   *"The injured Stuart line is gone."*
      – "Written by Somebody in the Window."

44   *"The Thames flows proudly to the sea,"*
      – 'Banks O' Nith.'

50   *"At length the lonely cot appears in view"*
      – 'The Cotter's Saturday Night.'

55   *"Had we never lov'd sae kindly..."*
      – 'Ae Fond Kiss, And Then We Sever.'

ACKNOWLEDGEMENTS

On behalf of the contributors to the book I would like to thank the following people without whose help and enthusiasm this book would not have been published in its present form.

Dumfries and Galloway Libraries
Dumfries and Galloway Regional Council
Economic Development Department
Janice
Alastair Johnston
Sandra Wilson
Shirley Bell
Liz Niven
Loftus Brown
Susanne Patterson
Tom Pow
Murdo Morrison
Hugh McIntyre
Malcolm Creedon
Solway Offset Services Limited
Remploy Creative Products
and
the Subscribers

John Clark

SUBSCRIBERS

1. Jack and Shirley Bell, Inveresk, Kelton, Dumfries
2. R and C E Ovens, Dumfries
3. James Swan, Mossdale
4. Tom and Isobel Evans, Marchmount, Dumfries
5. Dumfries and Galloway Libraries
6. Dumfries and Galloway Libraries
7. William B Hill, Eynhallow, Auldgirth
8. David Douglas, 6 Glencaple Avenue, Dumfries
9. David Douglas, 6 Glencaple Avenue, Dumfries
10. Tom Marchbank, Thornhill
11. Amy E McCubbin, Calside, Dumfries
12. R Stanley McEwan, Dumfries
13. Brian Johnstone, Stanbury, Dunscore. Dumfries
14. Mr and Mrs R Kennedy, Kelton, Dumfries
15. Margaret Binks, Rose Cottage, Crocketford
16. W Douglas Scott, Maxton, Roxburghshire
17. Andrew Gibson, 8 Hanover Close, Lochside Road, Dumfries
18. Keith Jewell, Ayr
19. A D Clark, Strawberrybank, Parkgate, Dumfries
20. Bill Parr, Halleaths, Lockerbie
21. Arthur C Thirwell, Flightline, Castle Douglas
22. Robert H C Stibbs, Dumfries
23. Jimmy and Kitty Kirkcaldy, Glencaple, Dumfries
24. Janet McCubbin [nee Clark], Perivale, Greenford, Middlesex
25. Carolyn Jane McCubbin, Stakeford Street, Dumfries
26. Jim and Cynthia Stewart, Castle Douglas
27. Edward Murray, Conheath, Glencaple, Dumfries
28. Janette D Murray, Conheath, Glencaple, Dumfries
29. James Scott, 4 Ivy Garth, Leeds
30. Jessica Armstrong, 1 Terregeles Street, Dumfries
31. Margaret Clark, Dumfries
32. Robert Clark Ross, Akron, Ohio, USA
33. Miller H Caldwell, Netherholm, Dumfries
34. Michael McCole, Dumfries
35. John B B Dodds, 244 Annan Road, Dumfries
36. P M Woodley, Dalry, Castle Douglas
37. Dorothy Boyes, Glebe Street, Dumfries
38. Joseph Jordan, Balmoral Road, Dumfries
39. Lisa M Brown, Barnton Road, Dumfries
40. Rev John R Smith, Paisley
41. Andrew Finnie, Newbridge, Dumfries
42. Elizabeth Miller, Springfield, Gretna
43. I Johnstone, 16 Roberts Crescent, Dumfries
44. Mr and Mrs David Goss, Broomrigg, Dumfries
45. Olive Little, Netherwood, Dumfries
46. Ann and Jimmy Brown, Kingholm Quay, Dumfries
47. Wilma R Paterson, Easdsle, Newbie, Annan
48. Ronald F Percy, Roughhills, Sandyhills
49. Janet M Machen, Knottinghley, Yorkshire
50. Major[retd] J G Carson, Dumfries
51. Warrant Officer D J Carson, Bergen, Germany
52. Police Sargeant S R Carson, Frimley, Surrey
53. Ms Christine Murray
54. Lesley Boyes, Castle Douglas
55. Alan G Brown, Heathhall, Dumfries
56. Jean McMurdo [Provost], Torwest, Torthorwald
57. Jean M Macfarlan, Georgetown, Dumfries
58. Stephen Alford, 8 Church Street, St Andrews, Fife
59. David and Suzanne Paterson, Heathhall, Dumfries
60. Catherine Haining, Glencaple, Dumfries
61. Andrew J Anderson, Dumfries
62. Athol Holton, Braithwaite, Cumbria

63   Pamela M Oliphant, Craigs Road, Dumfries.
64   Robert Dalgleish, Locharbriggs, Dumfries.
65   Thomas Blain, Heathhall, Dumfries.
66   John Howat, Newbridge, Dumfries.
67   Alan and Margaret Ramage, Dumfries.
68   W J Ramage, Ardwall Road, Dumfries.
69   Mrs Rena Blight, Oxenholme, Kendal.
70   George W S Park, Rockcliffe, Carlisle.
71   James W Huntly, Dumfries.
72   J A and J K Yeomans, Lincoln.
73   J A and J K Yeomans, Lincoln.
74   J A and J K Yeomans, Lincoln.
75   Councillor Robert Higgins, Dumfries and Galloway Council.
76   Patricia M Findlay, Newton Stewart, Wigtownshire.
77   Teresa Gooch, Dumfries.
78   Gina and Kieran, Nunholm Park, Dumfries.
79   Mr J Kenneth MacDonald.
80   William Stewart Hill, Minden Crescent, Dumfries.
81   Mary B Martin, Carlyle House, Ecclefechan.
82   Stuart Purdie, Peel Cottage, 22 Midtown, Dearham, Malyport, Cumbria. CA15 7HF.
83   Mr Thomas Allan, on the occasion of your 60th birthday from all the family.
84   Madeline M Davidson, Dumfries.
85   K M Carruthers, Dumfries.
86   Maureen Harkness, Heathhall, Dumfries.
87   Moyra F Stewart, Lockerbie.
88   Robert and Ruth Risien, Bonnyrigg, Midlothian.
89   Margaret J C Lessey, Newton Stewart, Galloway.
90   James C Halliday, Hawk Lea, Torthorwald.
91   Ian R F and Ian M Hamilton, Glencaple, Dumfries.
92   Mrs May Brown, Glenesslin Schoolhouse, Dunscore.
93   Robert W Tildesley, Moffat, Dumries.
94   Margaret I Latimer, 4 Seafield Road, Annan.
95   Martha W Smith.
96   Wm Cecil Syme, Kingholm Quay, Dumfries.
97   E Vivian Kerr, Glencaple Avenue, Dumfries.
98   J Knox, Dumfries.
99   E and W Wright, Georgetown, Dumfries.
100 Ruby McFarlane, Rothesay.
101 Elaine E McKay, Annan.
102 A and B McGroarly, Wetherby.
103 James G Marchbank, 8 Kingholm Drive, Dumfries.
104 Alison Findlater, 65 Princess Street, Lochmaben.
105 Heather M Findlater, 65 Princes Street, Lochmaben.
106 Neil McKay, Penpont.
107 Mr A Cameron, Crathie Avenue, Dumfries.
108 William S Gray, Kingholm Quay.
109 Mr and Mrs D Hermse, Princes Street, Grangemouth.
110 Gillian McNaught, Largs, Ayrshire.
111 Jean Lewis, Kirby-le-Soken.
112 G Wilson, 14 Robb Place, Castle Douglas.
113 Jean H Keiller, Corberry Mews, Dumfries.
114 Robert S Graham, Princes Court, Carlisle.
115 Mrs Anne C Carnochan, Cartha Place, Dumfries.
116 Carol K Thomson, 10 Hillview Avenue, Dumfries.
117 Mary Currie, Portland Drive, Dumfries.
118 Olive Graham, Closeburn, Thornhill.
119 Joanna Repton, Dunscore, Dumfries.
120 John Prott, Drongan, Ayrshire.
121 Mr J and Mrs M McAdam, 5 Linns Road, Torthorwald, Dumfries.
122 Mr G and Mrs L McAdam, 37 Inchewan, Birnam, Dunkeld, Perthshire.
123 Head Teacher, Dalbeattie High School, Dalbeattie.
124 Christine Harrion, Long Arrotts, Hemel Hempstead, Hertfordshire.

125 Elizabeth Haining, 74 Laghall Court, Kingholm Quay, Dumfries.
126 Ian A Whitehead, 9 Rowanbank Road, Dumfries.
127 Robert McGurn, Dumfries.
128 Ian Doole, Kilwinning, Ayrshire.
129 Mr and Mrs J McDonald, 1 Hannahfield Cottages, Glencaple Road, Dumfries. DG1 4TQ.
130 James Horsburgh, Aldershot, Hampshire.
131 Z Cameron, Annan.
132 Mary A Haythome, Barend, Sandyhills.
133 T H Bartlett, 17 Ewart Drive, Dumfries.
134 Richard and Helen Henderson, Glencaple, Dumfries.
135 George, Sheila and Stevan Clark, Dumfries.
136 Francis McBrine, Dumfries.
137 Annabella Gibson Goldielea Nursing Home.
138 Grace Gibson, Tweedville, Eastfield Road, Dumfries.
139 Bob and Betty Kerr, 7 Newdykes Road, Prestwick.
140 John Tokar.
141 Henry Jardine, (Love Mum, 1996).
142 Mr D Douglas, Dumfries.
143 Henry G Seabourne, Acocks Green, Birmingham.
144 Rebecca A MacDonald, Dumfries.
145 Robert McDennent, Craigie, Ayr.
146 Sheena Stewart, Arnside.
147 Evelyn and Sheilah Kirkpatrick, Cresswell Hill, Dumfries.
148 D C Smith, Burns Howff Club, Dumfries.
149 Mrs Linda T Green, Dumfries.
150 "Anon", Dumfries.
151 Gladys Hargreaves, Crossways, Wigtown.
152 Kathleen Noonan, Oakamoor, Staffordshire.
153 Tommy and Mary Motherwell, Durris Stables, Banchory.
154 David and Sandra Cullen, 36 Mossview, Dumfries.
155 Margaret T R Milroy.
156 William J Duff, Glencaple, Dumfries.
157 Isabella M Baker, Closeburn, Thornhill.
158 Isabella M Baker, Closeburn, Thornhill.
159 Christopher J Irving, Linfern Avenue, Kilmarnock.
160 Alex G MacEwen, Ayr.
161 W S Martindale, Ayr.
162 William A Earnshaw, Dumfries.
163 Margaret W Bryce, Lochside, Dumfries.
164 Murdo Morrison JP FSA Scot, President The Burns Federation, 110 Campbell Street, Wishaw. ML2 8HU.
165 Marion A Conaghan, Glencairn, Durnfries.
166 Isabelle P Hastings, Dunscore, Dumfries.
167 Agnes Glendinning, Dumfries.
168 Mrs C Wilson, Glencaple, Dumfries.
169 Mrs Doreen Gibson, Georgetown, Dumfries.
170 Mrs Nancy Risien, Dumfries.
171 A D Bell, 80 Pleasance Avenue, Dumfries.
172 Thomas Wilson MacFarlane, Addiewell Farm, West Calder.
173 Mrs E Wallace, Moffat Road, Dumfries.
174 Isobel D Woodburn, 'Braemar', Lockerbie.
175 Isobel D Woodburn, 'Braemar', Lockerbie.
176 Isobel D Woodburn, 'Braemar', Lockerbie.
177 Simon Goodwin, Sheffield.
178 John J Walsh, The Swallows, Dumfries.
179 Thomas Irvine, Troqueer, Dumfries.
180 —
181 Alison Morton-Cooper, Haugh of Urr, Castle Douglas.
182 Robert M Armstrong, Motherwell.
183 Robert M Armstrong, Motherwell.
184 Janett Patterson, Copland Street, Dalbeattie.
185 Patsy Shipsey, Stonehenge School, Amesbury, Salisbury.
186 Norma Oliver, Victoria Terrace, Dumfries.
187 Neil R Cole, Henry Street, Dumfries.

188 Maureen G McKerrow, Globe Inn, 56 High Street, Dumfries.
189 Mr and Mrs J M Pattison, Lochvale, Dumfries.
190 Richard and Anne Curran.
191 June Latimer - Happy Birthday from Peter and Pauline.
192 Murray Linton, Lovers Walk, Dumfries.
193 Ian Yates, St Albans and Aspen Crescent, Dumfries.
194 The Langholm Library Trust.
195 Gordon Millar, Newbridge, Dumfries.
196 Mr Douglas Carruthers and Mrs Elizabeth Carruthers, Ashleigh Green, Thornhill.
197 Hugh McIntyre, 18 Langlands, Dumfries.
198 Tom Pow, Springfield, Rosemount Street, Dumfries.
199 Loftus Brown, 4 Airds Avenue, Dumfries.
200 David M Hiddleston, Heathhall, Dumfries.
201 Lex Muir, Newton Stewart.
202 Miss Emma Davidson, Dumfries.
203 Derek W McKie, Georgetown Road, Dumfries.
204 Mrs A Stevenson, Lochmaben.
205 Alex and Linda Inman, Georgetown, Dumfries.
206 Mary K Knight, McLellan Street, Dumfries.
207 Margaret Annstrong Chambers, Dumfries.
208 Jimmy and Pat Smith, Scarboro, Canada.
209 A June Loxam.
210 John and Ruth Hattersley.
211 Robert Clark, Georgetown, Dumfries.
212 Douglas H B Crichton, 59 Victoria Street, Larkhall.
213 N C Craig Sharp, Edinburgh.
214 Catherine Ann Lee, Crieff.
215 Margaret Ross Ewart Hopkin.
216 Frame Manufacturers, Lochmaben, Lockerbie, Dumfriesshire.
217 Mr and Mrs P Matthews, Dalskairth Grange, Dalbeattie Road, Dumfries.
218 Kenneth and Mary Brown, Wickhouse.
219 Bill and Topsy, Gilloch Avenue.
220 Jack Groom, 33 Cartha Road.
221 Mr and Mrs Ian Smith, 9 Anne Arundel Court, Heathhall, Dumfries.
222 Mr and Mrs S Malone, Rotchell Park, Dumfries.
223 Happy Birthday Dad love from Lorna and Ian.
224 Happy Birthday Ian, all my love, Lorna.
225 City of Edinburgh Central Library.
226 To Ramsay and Lorraine from Andrew and Val.
227 To Dad, Many Happy Returns 30.5.96 From Brian and Liz.
228 Olly and Sandra Galligan, Dumfries.
229 June M Pringle.
230 Edward John Beckley.
231 Frank N Manson.
232 Mr and Mrs Beck, Dumfries.
233 To Mum and Dad, with love Shirley.
234 Kate, Stevie and Scott, Dumfries.
235 Gerald and Irene Dawson, Edinburgh.
236 Margaret E Brown, Mabie Court, Dumfries.
237 Sheila Mogg, Dumfries.
238 A. R. Johnston, Dumfries.
239 John and Margaret Murphie, Easdale, 20 Cartha Road, Dumfries
240 To David with love from Mum.
241 Alexander and Helen Baty, Elmbank Drive, Dumfries.
242 Dumfries and Galloway Libraries.
243 Dumfries and Galloway Libraries.
244 Dumfries and Galloway Libraries.
245 Dumfries and Galloway Libraries.
246 Dumfries and Galloway Libraries.
247 Dumfries and Galloway Libraries.

A WORD IN CONCLUSION

Although this book was compiled to pay homage to Scotland's National Poet on the bicentenary of his death, its purpose is not to recount his life as was. Scholars philosophers and academics far more qualified than I will write and re-write his story over and over. The book's main aim was to show that poetry can be, and still is, being written by working class people in the small part of Scotland that Robert Burns took to his heart. The beauty of its landscape, its people and his own working class roots inspired him to write poetry that will last forever. His genius will never fade.

The verses within this book were conceived and written by fellow Scots brought up in a working class environment similar in some ways to his own. The book shows that poetry can be used to describe almost anything we encounter in life. Whether it is used to depict the feelings generated by a beautiful landscape, or convey feelings of love or indeed horror, whether it is simply written just to bring a smile to our face as in 'The Ballad of Wullie Walker' is relatively unimportant. What is important is that poetry in whatever shape or form, is written from the heart.

JOHN CLARK